...st established
...el brands,
...s in travel.

...5 years our
...the secrets
...d the world,
... a wealth of
...on for travel.

**Rely on Thomas Cook as your
travelling companion on your next trip
and benefit from our unique heritage.**

Thomas Cook **pocket** guides

ZURICH

Written and updated by Teresa Fisher

Published by Thomas Cook Publishing
A division of Thomas Cook Tour Operations Limited
Company registration no. 3772199 England
The Thomas Cook Business Park, Unit 9, Coningsby Road,
Peterborough PE3 8SB, United Kingdom
Email: books@thomascook.com, Tel: +44 (0) 1733 416477
www.thomascookpublishing.com

Produced by Cambridge Publishing Management Limited
Burr Elm Court, Main Street, Caldecote CB23 7NU
www.cambridgepm.co.uk

ISBN: 978-1-84848-376-7

© 2007, 2009 Thomas Cook Publishing
This third edition © 2011 Thomas Cook Publishing
Text © Thomas Cook Publishing
Maps © Thomas Cook Publishing/PCGraphics (UK) Limited
Transport map © Communicarta Limited

Series Editor: Karen Beaulah
Production/DTP: Steven Collins

Printed and bound in Spain by GraphyCems

Cover photography © Charles O'Rear/CORBIS

CONTENTS

SYMBOLS KEY

The following symbols are used throughout this book:

ⓐ address ☏ telephone Ⓦ website address 🄻 opening times
Ⓝ public transport connections ❶ important

The following symbols are used on the maps:

𝑖	information office	▣	point of interest
✈	airport	○	city
➕	hospital	○	large town
🛡	police station	○	small town
🚌	bus station	═	motorway
🚆	railway station	—	main road
✝	cathedral	—	minor road
❶	numbers denote featured	—	railway
	cafés & restaurants		

Hotels and restaurants are graded by approximate price as follows:
£ budget price **££** mid-range price **£££** expensive

In addresses, 'Strasse' and '-strasse' (meaning 'street' or 'road')
are abbreviated to 'Str.' and '-str.'; 'Platz' and '-platz' (meaning
'square') are abbreviated to 'Pl.' and '-pl.'

▶ *The twin spires of Grossmünster*

INTRODUCING
Zurich

Introduction

There's more to Switzerland's largest city than gold bars and chocolate bars. It's a classical city with a contemporary edge, preserving its architectural and cultural heritage yet surprising the world with the latest innovations in art and architecture, fashion, shopping and design.

Forget the old image of a characterless and cold-hearted financial city of buttoned-up businessmen working in ubiquitous grey bank offices; of secret investment files and precision timing. Of course, the streets are meticulously clean and everything runs like clockwork, but it is also a fun-loving, dynamic and thriving metropolis. It is large enough to offer world-class facilities, but small enough to retain its Swiss charm and 19th-century intimacy.

Most of Zurich's sights fall within a compact, walkable area either side of the Limmat river, which bisects the city centre. The ancient hilly Niederdorf district to the east is a veritable labyrinth of ancient, cobbled lanes brimming with trendy bars, cafés and quirky shops. To the west, the Altstadt (Old Town) contains many of the city's finest historic buildings, and broad, leafy Bahnhofstrasse counts among the world's most sophisticated shopping boulevards. The trendy former industrial quarter of Zurich West reflects the city's radical change in recent years, while the lake, with its beautiful grassy parks and lakeside promenades, is framed by majestic, snow-capped mountains.

Located at the heart of Europe, today's Zurich cleverly combines the trams and architecture of Vienna, the waterways of Amsterdam, the street café society of Paris and the cobbled

old-town atmosphere of Stockholm into one delightful city.
Although not the nation's political capital, this heady mix –
together with a world-class art and music scene, the most
luxurious shopping in Europe and the infectious *joie de vivre*
of its people – demonstrates the city's position as Switzerland's
spiritual centre.

● *The Limmat cuts through the historic Altstadt*

When to go

SEASONS & CLIMATE

The city has four distinct seasons, each with a different appeal. Spring (March–May) is a lovely time to visit, before the summer crowds, and when the sweet-scented blossoms of the lime trees on Bahnhofstrasse are in bloom. The weather is mild but it can be rainy. Summer (June–August) is the perfect time to come, when the weather is at its finest and sunniest, although the city is at its busiest. The average summer temperature is around 22°C (71°F) and rarely rises above 30°C (86°F), and the humidity level is pleasant. A dip in the Limmat or the lake is always refreshing on warm days and balmy evenings. Autumn (September–November) is another popular time, with plenty of crisp, clear, sunny days. The city is quieter and there are excellent bargains in the shops.

● *Zürchers spill on to the streets during the summer*

During winter (December–February), once the thermometer falls below 0°C (32°F), the city is covered with a sugar-like sprinkling of snow. It is a magical time, with shop windows elaborately decorated and fairy lights illuminating the streets. However, the temperature usually ranges from a chilly –2°C (28°F) to just 4°C (39°F) by day (and it's even colder at night), so wrap up warmly.

ANNUAL EVENTS

February–March

ZüriCarneval The first major festival of the year is this wild carnival during Lent, with parades, fancy-dress, street entertainment and fireworks in the Niederdorf. Ⓦ www.zurichcarneval.ch

April

Sechseläuten (Six O'Clock Bells) marks the end of winter, when the working day traditionally ended with the church bells rather than at nightfall. The first ringing of the season celebrates the arrival of spring. A Procession of the Guilds (*Zug der Zünfte*) winds through the streets, involving around 7,000 participants, 500 horses, music ensembles and carriages. At 18.00 sharp, the guildsmen gallop round a giant bonfire by the lake and light the Böögg, a snowman-like figure made of straw and fireworks, who represents winter. It is said that the faster his head explodes, the better the summer will be. Ⓦ www.sechselaeuten.ch

June–July

The Zurich Festival is one of Europe's top festivals, with an extensive programme of opera, music, theatre and cultural exhibitions throughout the city. Ⓦ www.zuercher-festspiele.ch

July

Live at Sunset is the city's biggest open-air music festival. It takes place at the Dolder Eisbahn, on a hill with a magnificient view, and runs over two weeks. Previous line-ups have included such stars as Diana Ross and Simply Red. Ⓦ www.liveatsunset.ch

August

Street Parade In mid-August, nearly a million partygoers take to the streets for the colourful techno parade, with dancing day and night. Bigger than London's Notting Hill Carnival, it is Europe's largest annual street party. Ⓦ www.streetparade.ch

Theater Spektakel Held during the second half of August, the open-air, lakeside Theater Spektakel is among Europe's leading contemporary performing arts festivals.
Ⓦ www.theaterspektakel.ch

September

The Knabenschiessen (*Knabe* means boy) is one of the oldest events: a shooting competition for teenagers (girls included, since 1991, despite the name) on the Albisgütli, followed by the largest three-day fair in Switzerland. Ⓦ www.knabenschiessen.ch

September–October

Zurich Film Festival Founded in 2005, the Zurich Film Festival places particular emphasis on young, upcoming talent, and has become one of Europe's most important newcomers – within three years, the number of visitors shot to 27,000. With its red carpet and Hollywood stars, it rivals the traditional International Film Festival in Locarno. Ⓦ www.zurichfilmfestival.org

November

Expovina is the world's biggest wine-tasting show. It takes place aboard 12 boats on the lake and is a wonderful opportunity to taste some little-known Swiss wines. ⓦ www.expovina.ch

December

During Advent, there are plenty of Christmas concerts put on throughout the city and the aromas of gingerbread and *glühwein* (a type of mulled wine) fill the air. Christmas Markets sprout up all over, the one at the Hauptbahnhof (railway station) being Europe's largest covered market. One of the loveliest Christmas festivities is the **Lichterschwimmen**, when floating candles are launched from the Rathausbrücke into the river.

The new year is welcomed in with great revelry and dazzling fireworks by the lake at the nation's largest New Year's Eve party. ⓦ www.silvesterzauber.ch

PUBLIC HOLIDAYS

New Year's Day 1 Jan
Good Friday 22 Apr 2011; 6 Apr 2012; 29 Mar 2013
Easter Monday 25 Apr 2011; 9 Apr 2012; 1 Apr 2013
Ascension Day 2 June 2011; 17 May 2012; 9 May 2013
Whit Monday 13 June 2011; 28 May 2012; 20 May 2013
Bundesfeier (Swiss National Day) 1 Aug
Christmas Day 25 Dec
St Stephen's Day 26 Dec

Offices and shops are closed on national holidays (except at the Hauptbahnhof and the airport).

Dada

It may seem surprising that the outlandish, deliberately nonsensical Dada art movement was founded here in neutral, bourgeois Zurich. However, the city had long been a centre of artistic and liberal thought, attracting such scholars as Lenin, Jung, Joyce and Mann. Neutrality during World War I made Zurich a refuge for dissidents, and so Dadaism was founded in 1916 at Cabaret Voltaire (see page 82), a popular rendezvous for writers, painters and musicians. A rebellious antiwar movement and the very antithesis of conformity, it rejected the prevailing oppressive, materialistic standards in art by promoting a new 'anti-art'. The main exponents of the movement in Zurich included Hugo Ball, Tristan Tzara, Hans Arp and Emmy Hennings. Over the years, Dadaism gained support through public gatherings, discussion groups, readings and theatrical performances at Cabaret Voltaire. By 1920, the movement had reached its peak, and its influence reached beyond the visual and literary arts into 'Dada music', created by such composers as Erwin Schulhoff and Hans Heusser.

But Dadaism was not without its critics. A reviewer from the *American Art News* described it as 'the sickest, most paralyzing and most destructive thing that has ever originated from the brain of man'. Years later, even Dada artists described the movement as 'nihilistic... a phenomenon bursting forth in the midst of the post-war economic and moral crisis... a systematic work of destruction and demoralisation... embracing anarchy and the irrational.'

⬤ *Cabaret Voltaire is home to the Dadaist movement*

When World War I ended in 1918, many of the Zurich Dadaists returned to promote the movement in their home countries. Ironically, Dadaism went on to influence later, more positive art movements including Surrealism, Pop Art and Fluxus. Cabaret Voltaire fell into disrepair until it was occupied by a group claiming to be neo-Dadaists in 2002. After their eviction, the space reopened in 2004 as a museum dedicated to the history of Dada in Zurich.

History

Zurich's history dates back to 15 BC when a Roman customs post was established on the river on the site now called Lindenhof. They called it Turicum. The Romans built Zurich's first stone buildings and established a harbour and grapevines here. Around 250 people lived at Turicum, and you can see the remains of the ancient Roman baths through a metal grating in Thermengasse in the Altstadt. The Romans eventually withdrew from Zurich in 401 AD, to make way for the Franks and the Alemans. In 1218, Zurich was eventually recognized as a free city and was placed under the authority of the Holy Roman Emperor. To celebrate, the people of Zurich destroyed the Carolingian castle, using it as a quarry, and built the city's first Rathaus (town hall) on the banks of the Limmat river.

In 1336, nobleman Rudolf Brun, with the help of local craftsmen, ousted the city council from the Rathaus and founded the Constitution of the Guilds, thereby giving the city's artisans and traders economic and political power for several centuries. Brun made himself mayor and, during his rule, Zurich joined the Swiss Confederation in 1351 as the capital city of the canton of Zurich. The guilds remain active in society today.

During the Middle Ages, the Fraumünster was built as a convent for noblewomen, and the abbess was granted the right to hold markets, collect tolls and mint money. The Grossmünster was constructed, according to legend, by Charlemagne on the spot where Zurich's patron saints, the martyrs Felix and Regula, were buried (see page 80). Huldrych Zwingli, the first priest at the Grossmünster, initiated the Reformation from here in 1519.

His motto 'pray and work' was to have a profound effect on Zurich. In the second half of the 19th century, Alfred Escher, a trailblazer of modern Switzerland, built the Hauptbahnhof (main railway station) and founded the Swiss rail network, which revolutionized communications and made Zurich the nation's main transportation, research and business hub. It remained the country's political capital until 1848, when that honour was transferred to Bern.

Today Zurich remains the Swiss economic capital (half of the nation's income is generated here) and a major international financial centre. Many of the major Swiss banks have their headquarters here and it is home to the world's fourth-ranked stock market (after New York, Tokyo and London) and the largest gold bullion market. Combine this wealth and business prowess with a strong artistic and intellectual tradition, and a recent boom in gastronomy, dance clubs and popular culture, and it is not surprising that Zurich is considered to be one of the most stylish cities in Europe.

◒ *View over the rooftops of historic Zurich*

Lifestyle

Ever since the 1980s, when the Wohlgroth community squat gained notoriety by erecting a huge imitation railway station sign to greet inbound trains to the Hauptbahnhof, which read 'Zu Reich' ('too rich') rather than 'Zurich', people have been joking about the city's affluent lifestyle. But it *is* one of Europe's most expensive cities. The streets are not lined with gold, but there's plenty of it in the city vaults and, of the million or so people living in the canton of Zurich, a disproportionate number are millionaires.

Zurich is Switzerland's largest city, spread across 93 sq km (36 sq miles), and the city itself has a population of around 369,000. Only six per cent of Zürchers live in their own homes. The rest live in rented accommodation, as is the trend throughout Switzerland. Zurich is an important university city, with over 25,000 students in town, and foreigners have increased in recent years, now representing over a quarter of the population. This has also resulted in greater religious freedom. Most Zürchers speak a form of German called *Schwyzerdütsch* (Schweizer-Deutsch in standard German), with its own unique vocabulary, grammar and syntax.

Many Swiss stereotypes reign supreme here: everything runs like clockwork; everyone eats copious amounts of cheese and chocolate; the infamous 'gnomes' (as the British like to call Zurich's bankers) abound; and its citizens are generally law-abiding, efficient, hard-working, clean-living, polite and welcoming to visitors. Indeed, Zurich's hospitality is second to none, and around 75 per cent of employees work in the service sector.

But in recent years the laws have relaxed and so have the Zürchers. They work hard but they also play hard. The Swiss have access to a great health service, per capita earnings that are among the highest in the world and an outstanding education system. The local lifestyle is admired – and even envied – across the globe. It therefore comes as no surprise that, for seven years running, Switzerland's 'little big city' has been voted one of the world's top three places to live for quality of life (Mercer's 'Quality of Living' Survey).

▲ *Despite their reputation, Zürchers know how to relax*

Culture

For centuries, Zurich has had a strong artistic and intellectual tradition. It has long been a centre of liberal thought, attracting such scholars as Joyce, Mann, Jung, Lenin and Wagner. In 1916, the avant-garde Dadaist movement (see page 12) was born in the Niederdorf when a group of intellectuals rebelled against traditional artistic expression. Ever since, Zurich has been one of the global hubs of contemporary art, along with New York and London, and boasts more than 100 art galleries. Artistic excellence is maintained at the Kunsthaus, the city's foremost gallery, with its impressive collection of paintings and sculptures by Swiss and international masters, predominantly from the 19th and 20th centuries. The Migros Museum of Contemporary Art keeps abreast of the very latest trends, while the reopening of Cabaret Voltaire in 2004 marked the start of a brand new Dada era.

Zurich is also home to the largest number of museums in Switzerland and has more than 50 attractions revealing every aspect of Zürcher history and lifestyle, from toys to tourism. However, none provides better insight into local life than the Schweizerisches Landesmuseum (Swiss National Museum) with its remarkable and extensive collections spanning prehistory to the present day.

Visitors can enjoy concerts and music festivals throughout the year, ranging from small-scale open-air affairs to blockbuster pop events at the Hallenstadion. Opera is world class, with performances from September to May in the celebrated Opernhaus. During summer months, the lakeside open-air cinema is always hugely popular.

The Schweizerisches Landesmuseum charts the history of the Swiss people

Zurich is also undergoing a subcultural revolution, largely due to the reinvention of the formerly industrialised Züri-West district. New life has taken root within the old factory buildings, which now house a wide variety of hip bars and nightclubs. Best known is the trendy Schiffbau, an alternative venue for Zurich's main theatre. And the world-renowned techno Street Parade (see page 10), with 24-hour dancing in the streets, is now Europe's largest annual street party.

Zurich wears its history on its sleeve through its eclectic mix of architecture, from the photogenic, ancient buildings of the Altstadt, painted in ice-cream shades, to the city's immaculately restored guildhalls flanking the Limmat River, which provide rare insights into bygone city life. Le Corbusier's pavilion by the shores of the lake has left a legacy of 20th-century innovation while, more recently, the converted industrial spaces of Züri-West are supreme examples of postmodern industrial architecture.

For an excellent cultural overview of the city, consider a **guided cycle tour** (ⓦ www.zurichbybike.ch) or an 'ArchitecTour' (ⓦ www.zurichbybike.ch/architectour). Or if you're really brave, go on a **Ghost Walk** (ⓦ www.ghostwalk.ch), which delves into the city's past history to find its 'ghosts, ghouls and things that go yodel in the night'.

❾ *Ornate dome of the Grossmünster*

MAKING THE MOST OF
Zurich

Shopping

From beautifully hand-crafted Swiss-made articles to international luxury labels, shopping in Zurich inspires the fashion-conscious, delights lovers of tradition and never fails to excite souvenir hunters.

The main shopping district occupies a square kilometre at the heart of the city. This area contains everything, from Switzerland's most sophisticated department stores, tiny boutiques and quirky specialist shops to the haute couture of the world-famous shopping mile, the Bahnhofstrasse. While the vaults of gold that power Switzerland's financial centre lie beneath Bahnhofstrasse, at street level the affluent, fur-clad locals are happy to admire the opulent window displays and splash out on the designer clothes, watches, jewellery and chocolates of Zurich's most celebrated boutiques.

The 'in' districts of Sihl and Zurich West specialise in small, trend-setting boutiques, selling everything imaginable whether you're after interior design prototypes or funky shirts for men. Niederdorf contains a multitude of interior design shops and galleries, while the artisan quarter at Schipfe offers treasure troves of antiquities. The city enjoys a flourishing art trade, especially along the Rämistrasse 'art mile'.

Not only does Zurich offer stylish international brand names, it also presents its own urban labels, including Freitag bags (made from recycled truck tarpaulins), street-, beach- and snow-wear with urban attitude from Alprausch, effortlessly fashionable designer shirts by local designer Edo Popken, and sumptuous silk accessories at Fabric Frontline. There is also a bewildering choice of Swiss-made skis and snowboards, jewellery and watches. The finest local handicrafts can be found at Schweizer Heimatwerk. Failing that, there are plenty of nostalgic souvenir shops with amusing collections of beer steins, music boxes, Swiss knives, fondue pots, cuckoo clocks and cow bells.

Gourmets will enjoy the lavish international delicatessens at the Globus and Jelmoli department stores and the local fruit

⬤ *Where tradition meets modern*

USEFUL SHOPPING PHRASES

What time do the shops open/close?
Um wieviel Uhr öffnen/schließen die Geschäfte?
Oom veefeel oor erffnen/shleessen dee geshefter?

How much is this?	**Can I try this on?**
Wieviel kostet das?	Kann ich das anprobieren?
Veefeel kostet das?	*Can ikh das anprobeeren?*

My size is ...	**I'll take this one, thank you**
Ich habe Größe ...	Ich nehme das, danke schön
Ikh haber grersser ...	*Ikh neymer das, danker shern*

This is too large/too small/too expensive
Es ist zu groß/zu klein/zu teuer
Es ist tsu gross/tsu kline/tsu toyer

and vegetable market at Bürkliplatz on Tuesday and Friday mornings (which becomes a flea market on Saturdays). And don't even think of leaving Zurich without buying some chocolate, as it is *the* speciality here. It's hard to miss such celebrated chocolate shops as Sprüngli and Teuscher, with their mouthwatering window displays. Cheese is perhaps Switzerland's most famous export, and several specialist cheese shops offer everything from delicious mountain goats' cheeses to the runniest of *raclette* cheeses.

Eating & drinking

The food scene in Zurich has never been as exciting as it is now, with trendy eateries and world-class restaurants burgeoning throughout the city. There are now around 2,000 bars, cafés and restaurants serving a bewildering range of culinary delicacies from around the world, and a remarkable 400 of these serve guests outdoors in mild weather.

Whatever your taste and budget, Zurich has just the right eatery for you, from noodle bars, sausage stands and beer cellars to innovative gourmet temples inside former factory walls, lakeside fish restaurants and traditional guildhall establishments serving delicious Zurich specialities. Undoubtedly the most unusual dining experience is at Blinde Kuh (see page 89), the first restaurant in the world to be run by blind people, where you eat in total darkness. For a special occasion, Petermann's Kunststuben (see page 111) in nearby Küsnacht is Switzerland's top restaurant.

Traditional Swiss food is simple and hearty, relying heavily on dairy produce, and includes such humble mountain cuisine as *rösti* (crispy, fried, grated potato), cheese and meat fondues, *Älper Magrone* (macaroni cheese served with bacon, onions,

PRICE CATEGORIES
The ratings used in this book indicate the typical cost of a three-course meal for one person without drinks.
£ up to CHF 25   ££ CHF 25–75   £££ over CHF 75

● *Backstreet café in Niederdorf*

puréed apples and cinnamon) and *raclette* (melted cheese piled high on new potatoes, gherkins and pickled onions). The neighbouring countries of Austria, Germany, Italy and France have also influenced the local cooking, which in Zurich is frequently meat-heavy due to its proximity to Germany. And recently other world cuisines have gained a foothold, with fusion cuisine all the rage in the city's more fashionable restaurants. Vegetarian restaurants are also on the increase.

Zurich's culinary identity comes largely from its location on Lake Zurich. Its cuisine mixes typical country specialities with some excellent fish dishes too, including such delicacies as lake trout, bream, perch and anglerfish. The city's signature dish, however, is *Züri Gschnetzlets* (Swiss-German for *geschnetzeltes Kalbfleisch nach Zürcherart*, veal in a cream and mushroom sauce).

Look out also for *Leberknodli* (liver dumplings), potato croquettes, *Apfelkuechli* (fried apple slices), *Birchermüsli* (a delicious muesli, fruit and yoghurt mixture, generally eaten as a daytime snack or a light supper) and the ubiquitous *Apfelstrudel* (apple strudel), all commonplace on Zürcher menus.

Fine dining and fine wine go hand in hand in Zurich and there is no shortage of excellent Swiss wine to try. Some of the nation's best come from Valais and include *Fendant* (dry white) and *Dôle* (a smooth red). Zurich's vineyards are located mainly on the 'Gold Coast' of the lake's eastern shore. Look out for *Räuschling*, produced with exclusively Zürcher grapes, and local *Schiterberger* and *Gamaret* reds. For spirits, try *Schnapps*, *Kirsch* (cherry spirit) or *Xellent*, a triple-distilled vodka made with high-quality Swiss rye and alpine glacier water.

EATING OUT

Eating out is very popular in Zurich and so it is advisable to make a reservation. In cafés, tearooms, beer halls and less expensive restaurants, table sharing is common. Food is typically served 12.00–14.00 and 18.00–21.00 (22.00 at weekends).

By law, restaurants have to display their menus and prices outside, so the price you see is the price you pay (it already includes a service charge of 15 per cent), and tipping is therefore not normally necessary. However, locals often round up the bill. The *Tagesmenu* (menu of the day), usually comprising two or even three courses, can be excellent value.

USEFUL DINING PHRASES

I would like a table for ... people, please
Ich möchte einen Tisch für ... Personen, bitte
Ikh merkhter inen teesh foor ... perzohnen, bitter

Waiter/waitress!	**May I have the bill, please?**
Herr Ober/Frau Kellnerin!	Die Rechnung, bitte?
Hair ohber/frow kell-nair-in!	*Dee rekhnung, bitter?*

I am a vegetarian. Does this contain meat?
Ich bin Vegetarier (Vegetarierin *fem.*). Enthält das hier Fleisch?
Ish bin veggetaareer (veggetaareerin). Enthelt dass heer flyshe?

Where is the toilet (restroom), please?
Wo sind die Toiletten, bitte?
Voo zeent dee toletten, bitter?

If a picnic lunch is more your style, make a beeline for the fabulous delicatessens in the basements of the Jelmoli and Globus department stores, the fruit and vegetable market at Bürkliplatz (Tuesday and Friday mornings), and local bakeries and cheese shops to stock up on provisions. The most popular picnic venue is the grassy lakeside but, for the energetic, the top of Uetliberg (Uetli Mountain) is undoubtedly the prime spot where your climbing efforts will be rewarded by a stunning view over the city.

Entertainment & nightlife

Forget yodelling, alphorns and other types of traditional Swiss entertainment. Zurich is considerably less conservative than it was 15 years ago and nights are now long and sophisticated with over 500 cool, stylish bars, clubs and discos to choose from, many in the Niederdorf and Züri-West quarters. Weekends begin on Thursdays and the city's flamboyant club scene caters to all tastes, although Latin, Techno and House beats take centre stage at present. That said, compared with people in other major European cities, most Zürchers are not night owls. Only a handful party till dawn, and many of the nightspots close down around 01.00 or 02.00 (later at weekends).

In the city centre, sophisticated chill-out bars draw the beautiful people, while most of the gay clubs and bars are located in the Niederdorf quarter, together with a handful of raucous beer cellars. This is also the most likely district to find buskers and other street performers. During summer, when the sun goes down things start to hot up at the city's pools and lidos, with their dreamy open-air bars idyllically located on the banks of the Limmat and the lake. The newly hip former industrial quarter of Züri-West has a special buzz about it, with its thriving subculture and its old factories converted into bars, clubs and leisure venues. The city also boasts numerous live music haunts, ranging from mellow, intimate jazz bars and witty oom-pah bands in beer cellars to huge rock and pop arenas, featuring artists from all over the world.

On the cultural front, Zurich offers a prestigious programme of performing arts and cultural events throughout the year.

The main venue for classical music is the impressive Tonhalle with its superb acoustics, while the opera and ballet productions at the Opernhaus (Opera House) enjoy a worldwide reputation. Throughout the year, chamber concerts and recitals are staged in churches and museums, and in summer you'll find performances in some of the city parks.

The city's theatre programme is unlikely to appeal to visitors, unless you speak German, in which case there is the full spectrum on offer, from classical to avant-garde and even a **puppet theatre for children** (ⓦ www.theater-stadelhofen.ch). Cinema, however, is a different matter, with most screenings shown in the original

⬥ *The Zurich Opera House hosts world-class productions*

LISTINGS

The best source of local entertainment listings is the daily newspaper *Tages Anzeiger* (available from newsstands); its weekly 'Züritipp' section previews cinema, theatre, music and nightlife. There are also listings in the daily *Neue Zürcher Zeitung* (NZZ), while the monthly magazine *Swiss News* (available in newsagents and English bookshops) documents what's on in English. The Tourist Office is an excellent source of cultural knowledge, with its useful event calendar and nightlife information, detailed on the website ⓦ www.zuerich.com. For further nightlife and cultural info, grab one of the free papers (*20 Minuten* or *Blick am Abend*), in German, found in boxes at tram and train stations. You can also check out the online event guide at ⓦ www.zueritipp.ch

version with subtitles. Open-air cinema is especially popular in summer, when giant screens are erected by the lake and river. Check the website ⓦ www.orangecinema.ch for further info.

Tickets are best purchased from the relevant box office at each venue. Alternatively, book by phone or via the Internet at ⓦ www.ticketcorner.com, ⓦ www.starticket.ch. The **Hauptbahnhof Tourist Office**'s cultural information desk (ⓘ 044 215 40 00 ⓦ www.zuerich.com) and the department stores **Jelmoli** (see page 71) and **Migros** (ⓐ Löwenstr. 31 ⓦ www.migros.ch) also offer advance bookings for theatre, musicals, opera, classical concerts, cabaret and other events.

Sport & relaxation

PARTICIPATION SPORTS

One of the joys of Zurich is its proximity to nature, with the river, the lake and the majestic mountains all on the doorstep. With that much nature on offer, Zürchers enjoy a healthy outdoor lifestyle, including the following popular activities:

Boating

Hire a pedalo or a motorboat from various locations around the lake.

Cycling

Throughout the summer season, Zürirollt offers free bike hire from stalls at the Hauptbahnhof, Globus-City and the Opera House (for details, see page 53). ⓦ www.zuerirollt.ch

In-line skating

Tour the lake, and join the infamous **Monday Night Skate** (ⓐ Departs from Bürklipl. ⓦ www.nightskate.ch ⓛ Every second Monday, spring–autumn) or the Swiss In-line Cup, the world's largest in-line marathon.

Swimming

Take a dip in the lake, the river or one of the many pools and lidos around the city (ⓦ www.badi-info.ch/zueri-badis.html). Alternatively, head to Alpamare (see page 106), the largest indoor water park in Europe.

Volleyball
There's beach volleyball during summer at the Flussbad Obere Letten lido.

Walking
Stroll along the lake, climb Uetliberg (see page 65) or hike in the wooded hills of the picture-postcard Zürcher Oberland region.

Winter sports
Top ski resorts such as Davos, Klosters, Flims and Laax are just a two-hour train ride away, and all easily accessible from the Hauptbahnhof (change in Landquart for Davos and Klosters; Chur for Flims and Laax), as are some smaller, lesser-known resorts, including Hoch Ybrig (see page 111) and Flums (change in Ziegelbrücke or Sargans), all within quick and easy reach.

SPECTATOR SPORTS
Zurich's sporting events attract visitors from around the world. Many take place at the **Hallenstadion** (ⓦ www.hallenstadion.ch ⓝ S-Bahn: Bahnhof Oerlikon). Tickets are available from the box office or online at ⓦ www.ticketcorner.com

Football
Zurich is the FIFA headquarters and occasionally hosts international football matches.

Freestyle.ch
An event showcasing tricks in snowboarding, free-skiing and skateboarding. ⓐ Landiwiese ⓦ www.freestyle.ch

Ice hockey

The local team ZSC Lions plays at the Hallenstadion. Matches are played throughout the winter season and are always a thrill to watch. ⓐ Hallenstadion ⓦ www.zsclions.ch

Ice skating

Art on Ice is a glitzy show performed by international figure skaters in February. ⓐ Hallenstadion ⓦ www.artonice.ch

Marathon

The international Zurich Marathon, the largest in Switzerland, takes place in April. ⓦ www.zurichmarathon.ch

🔺 *Runners in the Zurich Marathon*

Accommodation

Swiss hospitality is world renowned, and Zurich has over 120 hotels ranging from 5-star deluxe and chic boutique hotels to simple guesthouses and youth hostels. Finding accommodation can be difficult, so try to reserve in advance.

As a general rule, the closer to the lake, the pricier the accommodation. The atmospheric Altstadt also commands high prices for its traditional ambience. More affordable hotels can be found in some of the backstreets, and especially in Niederdorf, although this quarter can be rather lively at night. Some of the cheapest accommodation is in trendy Zurich West.

City Backpacker £ A lively, international atmosphere greets you at this centrally placed youth hostel with private rooms, family rooms, dormitories and self-catering facilities.
⊘ Niederdorfstr. 5 (Niederdorf & beyond) ⓣ 044 251 90 15
Ⓦ www.city-backpacker.ch

Comfort Inn Royal £ Friendly, stylish business accommodation in the city centre. ⊘ Leonhardstr. 6 (Central Zurich) ⓣ 044 266 59 59
Ⓦ www.comfortinn.ch

PRICE CATEGORIES
The ratings used in this book indicate the typical cost of a double room with breakfast for one night.
£ up to CHF 250   ££ CHF 250–400   £££ over CHF 400

Leoneck £ An offbeat, fun choice, decorated in 'Swiss ethno' style. The rooms have original wall paintings by local artists, and there are cow motifs everywhere. Superb value. ⓐ Leonhardstr. 1 (Niederdorf & beyond) ⓣ 044 254 22 22 ⓦ www.leoneck.ch

Limmathof £ Simple, clean and excellent value, this centrally located hotel also contains a Swiss-style restaurant and a vegetarian restaurant. ⓐ Limmatquai 142 (Niederdorf & beyond) ⓣ 044 267 60 40 ⓦ www.limmathof.com

X-TRA £ At the heart of the trendy Züri-West district, this Bauhaus hotel adjoining the city's largest nightclub appeals to a young crowd. ⓐ Limmatstr. 118 (Zurich West) ⓣ 044 448 15 95 ⓦ www.x-tra.ch

City ££ Just around the corner from Bahnhofstrasse, with 64 smart, modern rooms, budget prices and a pleasant roof terrace.

⬤ *The classy exterior of the Widder Hotel*

ⓐ Löwenstr. 34 (Central Zurich) ⓣ 044 217 17 17
ⓦ www.hotelcity.ch

Greulich ££ A boutique hotel, with minimalist furnishings and neutral colour schemes by Jean Pfaff, a Swiss artist known for his monochromatic art. The 18 rooms are clustered around inner courtyard gardens. ⓐ Herman Greulich-Str. 56 (Central Zurich) ⓣ 043 243 42 43 ⓦ www.greulich.ch

Helmhaus ££ A friendly Niederdorf hotel combining traditional hospitality with modern comforts (including Wi-Fi throughout). Ask for a room overlooking the river. ⓐ Schifflände 30 (Niederdorf & beyond) ⓣ 044 266 95 95 ⓦ www.helmhaus.ch

Lady's First Design Hotel ££ This stucco-fronted 19th-century villa near the lake once accommodated country girls at finishing school. Today its original features combine with chic, 21st-century décor. Facilities include a wellness centre (for women only) and a fabulous roof terrace. ⓐ Mainaustr. 24 (Niederdorf & beyond) ⓣ 044 380 80 10 ⓦ www.ladysfirst.ch ⓝ Tram: 4 (Feldeggstrasse)

Romantik Florhof ££ A romantic boutique hotel with just 35 rooms in a former 15th-century merchant's home, in a tranquil, leafy setting near the Kunsthaus. ⓐ Florhofgasse 4 (Niederdorf & beyond) ⓣ 044 250 26 26 ⓦ www.florhof.ch

Rössli ££ Ultra-small, stylish and affordable, this is a favourite with hip business travellers. Contemporary white-on-white

décor and a charming roof terrace overlooking the old town.
ⓐ Rössligasse 7 (Niederdorf & beyond) ⓣ 044 256 70 50
ⓦ www.hotelroessli.ch

Seefeld ££ State-of-the-art technology and design are the
hallmarks of this trendy hotel, near the Opera House, the lake
and Bellevue. The bar draws the beautiful people of Zurich
and there is also a roof terrace, Wi-Fi access throughout and
a small gym. ⓐ Seefeldstr. 63 (Niederdorf & beyond) ⓣ 044 387 41
41 ⓦ www.hotel-seefeld.ch

Town House ££ A modern boutique hotel with just 21 rooms in
the style of an English townhouse, well placed just a stone's
throw from the Hauptbahnhof (main train station).
ⓐ Schützengasse 7 (Central Zurich) ⓣ 044 200 95 95
ⓦ www.townhouse.ch

Seidenhof ££–£££ Just off Bahnhofstrasse, this highly functional
yet stylish hotel was once an important centre for the city's silk
trade. Facilities include Wi-Fi and high-speed Internet access in
all rooms, a minimalist, modern-Asian restaurant and a massage
centre. ⓐ Sihlstr. 9 (Central Zurich) ⓣ 044 228 75 00
ⓦ www.seidenhof.ch; www.the-massage-therapy.ch

Uto Kulm ££–£££ For a truly tranquil retreat, escape the city
bustle and stay in a car-free zone on Uetliberg, the so-called
'Top of Zurich' (see page 65). Design is paramount in this classy,
minimalist hotel with its breathtaking vistas. For that special
occasion, you can reserve a luxurious 'romantic' suite: the Tower

Suite has a wood-burning stove and a heart-shaped whirlpool bath. ⓐ Uetliberg (Central Zurich) ⓣ 044 457 66 66 ⓦ www.utokulm.ch

Baur au Lac £££ Among Switzerland's grandest hotels, in an unsurpassed location adjoining Bahnhofstrasse and with a private park by the lake, this traditional, family-run hotel has welcomed such luminaries as Wagner, Liszt and Lennon since its opening in 1844. ⓐ Talstr. 1 (Central Zurich) ⓣ 044 220 50 20 ⓦ www.bauraulac.ch

Dolder Grand £££ High in the hills northeast of Zurich, this deluxe 5-star spa hotel affords magnificent lake and alpine views, plus easy access (via hotel shuttle bus) to the city centre. ⓐ Kurhausstr. 65 (Niederdorf & beyond) ⓣ 044 456 60 00 ⓦ www.thedoldergrand.com

Widder £££ Just off Bahnhofstrasse, this striking, luxury hotel in the Altstadt consists of ten ancient interlinked townhouses, cleverly fused together by Zurich artist Tilla Theuss. Think ancient frescoes, exposed bricks and wooden beams brilliantly juxtaposed with glass and chrome, plus a rooftop terrace with spectacular views, and a chic jazz bar. ⓐ Rennweg 7 (Central Zurich) ⓣ 044 224 25 26 ⓦ www.widderhotel.ch

Zum Storchen £££ One of Zürich's grand traditional-style hotels, renowned for its hospitality for over six centuries, and the only hotel located directly on the Limmat River. ⓐ Am Weinplatz 2 (Central Zurich) ⓣ 044 227 27 27 ⓦ www.storchen.ch

THE BEST OF ZURICH

Zurich is compact, and both easy and enjoyable to explore on foot, thanks to its beautiful lake, elegant streets, graceful spires and its maze of cobbled alleyways fringing the river. Most main sights lie in and around the car-free Altstadt and Niederdorf. The remainder are easily accessible by tram.

TOP 10 ATTRACTIONS

- **Schweizerisches Landesmuseum** Make this fascinating museum your first port of call. Once you have a grasp of the nation's colourful history, walks around town are all the more rewarding (see page 97).

- **Kunsthaus** Switzerland's top art gallery spans the centuries from the Middle Ages to the present day, but specialises in 19th- and 20th-century Swiss art (see page 84).

- **Fraumünster** Renowned for its five world-famous stained-glass windows by Chagall, which together represent a lavish fusion of colour and ethereality (see page 63).

- **Bahnhofstrasse** The city's main thoroughfare, a shoppers' paradise and the most overt manifestation of the country's wealth (see page 59).

- **Lake Zurich** An idyllic setting for boating, swimming, walking, picnicking or simply relaxing on the grassy banks (see pages 102–13).

- **Niederdorf** This ancient quarter, distinguished by its picturesque cobbled streets, tiny specialist shops, bars and restaurants, is especially atmospheric by night (see pages 76–91).

- **Grossmünster** The city's cathedral and the birthplace of the Swiss Reformation. Climb the tower for the best aerial views of the city (see page 77).

- **Altstadt** The city's most charming quarter, with its steep, cobbled lanes, beautiful mansions and tranquil, shady squares (see page 58).

- **Migros Museum für Gegenwartskunst** Extraordinary paintings, sculpture and photography by the top trend-setters in contemporary art, housed in a former brewery (see page 96).

- **Uetliberg** Affectionately called the 'Top of Zurich', Uetli Mountain has sensational 360°-views of the city, the lake and the Alps (see page 65).

Graffiti adorns the former industrial sites of Zurich West

Suggested itineraries

HALF-DAY: ZURICH IN A HURRY

If you only have a few hours, start at the Hauptbahnhof and stroll along the celebrated Bahnhofstrasse, admiring the glittering window displays. Stop for coffee at Sprüngli in Paradeplatz before heading down to the lake to glimpse the city's snow-capped, mountainous backdrop. Head back along the river to visit the Fraumünster with its dazzling stained-glass windows by Chagall, or the Grossmünster on the east bank of the Limmat, before enjoying a snack in a typical Zurich café.

1 DAY: TIME TO SEE A LITTLE MORE

After you have completed the recommended half-day sightseeing, add a museum visit to your itinerary. The Schweizerisches Landesmuseum provides a fascinating historical background to the city, while the Kunsthaus is the city's finest gallery. Spend the rest of the day exploring Niederdorf, dipping into its delightful quirky boutiques and trendy cafés and bars, before enjoying a sumptuous dinner in one of the ancient guildhall restaurants.

2–3 DAYS: TIME TO SEE MUCH MORE

The extra days provide plenty of time to explore the lake. Stroll along the east bank and take time out to watch the world go by. Then take a boat trip for a new perspective of the city. Alternatively, take in another museum – modern art lovers in particular will enjoy the Migros Museum for Contemporary Art – or climb to the summit of Uetliberg, Zurich's very own mountain. You'll also have time to eat some chocolate, buy some souvenirs and check out the city's nightlife.

LONGER: ENJOYING ZURICH TO THE FULL

A longer stay enables you to soak up the café culture of Niederdorf, appreciate the relaxed yet efficient lifestyle of the Zürchers, and enjoy the sun in the city's legendary lidos. You could also take at least one trip out of town (see pages 102–24).

⬥ *The Grossmünster dominates the Zurich skyline*

Something for nothing

Strapped for cash in one of the world's most expensive cities? Don't worry! There are plenty of sights and attractions to amuse you, without placing demands on your wallet.

Art aficionados on a budget need not be disappointed in Zurich, as many of the museums and galleries are free, including the Helmhaus (see page 83) and the Spielzeugmuseum (Toy Museum, see page 130). Even the beautiful Botanischer Garten, the *pièce de résistance* of all the city parks and gardens, is free (see page 76).

For a taste of historic Zurich, explore the Altstadt, where the hilly, cobbled streets are lined with romantic, shuttered houses, many painted in pastel shades and adorned with cascading geraniums. Don't forget to admire the interiors of the magnificent churches (most are free, though you may have to pay to go up their towers). Then soak up the atmosphere and people-watch in the sociable Niederdorf quarter (see pages 76–91). Better still, why not explore the city on a free hired bike (see page 53)?

Zurich is a shopper's paradise and, even if you can't afford the shops' contents, you should certainly spend time admiring their window displays, particularly in the grand Bahnhofstrasse.

On a fine day, there is nothing more enjoyable than walking along the quaysides of the Limmat and the lake. The lake draws visitors and locals alike to its shores to relax, snooze, sunbathe or simply watch the world go by. In summer months, it's even warm enough for swimming. Stroll along its western shore and before long you'll be out in the countryside. Or, if you're feeling really energetic, climb to the top of Uetliberg for stunning views of the city and the Alps and a picnic spot to take your breath away.

If you're lucky, you may experience one of Zurich's 'free' street parties (see pages 9–10), should your visit coincide with one of the annual celebrations for Carnival, Sechseläuten or New Year, or the massive Street Parade in August.

Finally, who says everything in Switzerland is expensive? Zurich serves free drinks... from its 1,200 ornamental drinking fountains! They all provide free water to quench your thirst after a long, hot, 'free' day of sightseeing.

○ The Helmhaus holds free exhibitions of cutting-edge art

When it rains

The bad news is that it can rain in Zurich at any time of year. But the good news is that there are plenty of attractions catering for all ages and interests to keep you amused in the heaviest downpour or even in a winter snowstorm.

For starters, why not take a guided Classic Trolley Tour of the city? It's a great way to get your bearings, to learn a little about

● Hop on a trolley for a whistle-stop tour of the city

the history and lifestyle of the Zürchers, and to sightsee
under cover.

Avoid the showers by visiting one of over a hundred museums
and galleries catering for all ages and interests, from high-brow
contemporary art to toy, chocolate and watch museums. At
the Kunsthaus, Zurich's premier art gallery, the sun-drenched
Impressionist landscapes of Monet, Cézanne and Van Gogh are
bound to brighten the rainiest of days. Or seek refuge from the
elements in the city's magnificent churches. The Fraumünster is
best known for its stunning Chagall stained-glass windows,
while the Grossmünster, the city's cathedral, is austere but
grandiose.

Zurich's shopping ranks among the best in the world, and
there are several large department stores in and around
Bahnhofstrasse (including Globus, Jelmoli, Grieder and Manor)
to occupy keen shoppers for hours.

Children young and old will love a visit to Zoo Zurich (see
page 81) even in the rain; there are numerous indoor displays,
which include a spectacular rainforest with its own tropical
microclimate. Alpamare (see page 106), the largest covered
aquatic park in Europe, with its massive tangle of slides,
whirlpools and thermal pools, is also an ideal family outing
when it's wet.

If that sounds too energetic, join locals for the fine Zurich
tradition of coffee and cake mid-morning, mid-afternoon or
indeed at any time. Sprüngli at Paradeplatz or Café Schober in
Niederdorf are two of the best-loved venues. And in the evening,
take your pick of trendy designer bars, cosy, old-fashioned beer
cellars or intimate, candlelit traditional pubs.

On arrival

TIME DIFFERENCES
Swiss clocks follow Central European Time (CET). During
Daylight Saving Time (end Mar–end Oct), the clocks are put
forward one hour.

ARRIVING
By air
Zurich's **Kloten Airport** (Ⓦ www.zurich-airport.com),
Switzerland's largest international airport, has excellent
facilities and shopping.

    The airport is located 11 km (7 miles) north of the city. The 24-
hour taxi service to the city centre is expensive (around CHF 60).
Alternatively, there is a train every 10 minutes to the Hauptbahnhof
(main station), operating 05.00–24.00 daily, which takes around
20 minutes and costs around CHF 6.20. Some hotels offer
a direct airport shuttle service.

By rail
The swift, punctual Swiss railway network provides easy access
to the city and enjoyable, stress-free excursions further afield.
More than 1,900 trains stop at the Hauptbahnhof daily from
all over Europe (ticket office 🕐 05.30–23.15).

By road
Zurich's main **bus station** is located at Sihlquai (ⓐ Ausstellungsstr. 15
❶ 044 434 4111), just behind the Hauptbahnhof. An efficient bus
network connects all the main cities in Switzerland and abroad.

Driving in Switzerland is relatively straightforward and Zurich is easily accessed via the A1 from Bern (to the west) or St Gallen (to the east).

FINDING YOUR FEET

Despite first impressions of an ultra-efficient, spick-and-span city, the pace of life in Zurich is surprisingly relaxed and the people are friendly and happy to help. It's safe with a low crime rate but there are incidents of petty crime, so do take common-sense precautions (see Health, safety & crime, page 128), especially in Zurich West and at the northern end of Niederdorf.

ORIENTATION

The city is divided into districts, each with its own distinctive characteristics. Many quarters are pedestrianised, including Bahnhofstrasse, Zurich's most celebrated shopping boulevard.

● The Hauptbahnhof, Zurich's main train station

IF YOU GET LOST, TRY ...

Excuse me, do you speak English?
Entschuldigen Sie, sprechen Sie Englisch?
Entshuldigen zee, shprekhen zee english?

Excuse me, is this the right way to the old town/the city centre/the tourist office/the station/the bus station?
Entschuldigung, geht es hier zur Altstadt/zur Stadtmitte/zur Touristeninformation/zum Bahnhof/zum Busbahnhof?
Entshuldeegoong, gayt es here tsoor altshtat/tsoor shtatmitter/zur Touristeninformatsion/tsoom baanhof/tsoom busbaanhof?

Lose yourself in the labyrinth of narrow streets and alleys of the Altstadt (on the west bank of the Limmat) or Niederdorf (on the east bank); there are city maps at the tram stops, and a host of unmissable landmarks (such as the river, the lake, and the spires of the Grossmünster, Fraumünster and St-Peterskirche) to help you keep your bearings. And if you do get lost, just ask for help – people are generally friendly and happy to assist.

GETTING AROUND

Zurich's public transport system is operated by **VBZ Züri-Linie** (Zurich Public Transport ☎ 0848 988 988 ⓦ www.vbz.ch). The ticket systems of all public transport in the canton are linked together, which means you only need one ticket whether you travel by tram, bus, boat or train (S-Bahn).

By tram & bus

The extensive, efficient network of trams and buses runs daily from around 05.30 to 00.30, depending on the route. You must buy a ticket before you embark, or you may be fined. Many different types of ticket are available, including a *Kurzstrecke*, valid for a trip of up to four stops, and a *Tageskarte*, which is valid for one day.

By bicycle

Zürirollt (🕒 08.00–21.30 Ⓦ www.zuerirollt.ch) offers free bike hire, from small stands located outside the Hauptbahnhof and from Globus-City and the Bürkliplatz (09.00–21.30 May–Oct).

By boat

Zürichsee Schifffahrt (Ⓦ www.zsg.ch) operates lake cruises from Bürkliplatz Pier throughout the year, as well as speciality cruises,

---

ZürichCARD

If you are staying in the city for a couple of days and plan to sightsee, consider getting a ZürichCARD, which offers unlimited travel by tram, bus, train, boat, cable car and funicular, free entry to all city museums, and a host of other attractive offers and discounts. Twenty-four and seventy-two hour versions are available and can be purchased from VBZ ticket booths, train stations, the airport, major hotels and the Tourist Information Office in the Hauptbahnhof. The ticket becomes valid once you stamp it in one of the ticket machines at a transport stop. Ⓦ www.zuerich.com

> **DRIVING IN SWITZERLAND**
> *Vignettes* (annual motorway tax discs) cost around CHF 40
> and are available online from the **Switzerland Travel
> Centre** in London (☎ 0207 420 4934
> 🖥 www.swisstravelsystem.co.uk) or from border customs
> offices, service stations, garages and post offices in
> Switzerland. Failure to display one on a motorway can
> result in a hefty fine.

which include a sunset cruise, a summer brunch boat and a winter
fondue boat. **Limmatschifffahrt** (🖥 www.zvv.ch) plies up the
Limmat from Bürkliplatz Pier to the Landesmuseum twice an
hour from April to October.

By car

There is little need for a car in Zurich, since the public transport
system is so reliable and efficient. City-centre parking is scarce
and expensive.

CAR HIRE

It is only worthwhile hiring a car if you are heading out of town
to explore the countryside. There are several car hire companies
at the airport.

Avis ☎ 044 800 77 33 🖥 www.avis.ch
Budget ☎ 044 800 77 33 🖥 www.budget.ch
Europcar ☎ 043 255 56 56 🖥 www.europcar.ch

▶ *The Limmat flowing past the Fraumünster*

THE CITY OF
Zurich

Central Zurich

Central Zurich is the district of high finance and elegant shops, centred around the celebrated Bahnhofstrasse, one of Europe's most prestigious streets, where all Zürchers come to promenade and shop. Clinging to the banks of the Limmat, the neighbouring, car-free Altstadt is the oldest part of town, with its delightful cobbled lanes and luxury boutiques. The entire district is dominated by its spires – the slender green spire of Fraumünster and the graceful spire of St-Peterskirche, featuring the largest clock face in Europe.

SIGHTS & ATTRACTIONS

Altstadt (Old Town)

The early medieval Old Town flanks the Limmat and is characterised by a cobweb of picturesque lanes, steep cobbled alleyways and hidden sun-splashed squares. The streets are lined with romantic, ancient houses, many adorned with cascading geraniums. Highlights include: Lindenhof, the former Roman customs post; Weinplatz, the oldest market square; Thermengasse, an alley constructed over an excavated Roman bath; Augustinergasse, a street with attractive oriel windows; Münsterhof, the grandest square; and Münzplatz, overlooked by the Augustinerkirche, an austere but beautiful church that was secularised for a while during the Reformation for use as the town's mint. ◔ Tram: 6, 7, 11, 13 (Rennweg); Tram: 2, 6, 7, 8, 9, 11, 13 (Paradeplatz)

Bahnhofstrasse

Bahnhofstrasse is reputed to have the most expensive real-estate prices in the world. However, it is perhaps best known for its shopping. Indeed, this car-free shopping mile symbolises everything Zurich represents: elegance and prestige, quality, financial prowess and economic diversity. It leads from the Hauptbahnhof (main railway station) to Lake Zurich, and follows the ancient course of the western city wall, past some of the most exclusive jewellers, watchmakers and fashion boutiques in the world.

● *A characteristic Altstadt building*

A GOLDEN CITY

There's no denying that Switzerland is an affluent nation and it's in Zurich that the serious money begins. Most major Swiss banks have their headquarters in and around Paradeplatz, and Zurich is the world's largest gold market. When you stroll up wealthy Bahnhofstrasse you're actually walking on gold. Admittedly, the street is not paved with it but, immediately beneath your feet, the massive bank vaults are full of gold ingots.

Two-thirds of the way along lies Paradeplatz (Parade Square), the scene of a medieval market until the 19th century, when it became the main venue for military processions. Nowadays it is the modern centre of the city, a major tram intersection and the main location of Sprüngli, the city's most celebrated confectioner. The bars and cafés here offer some of the best people-watching in town.

Bahnhofstrasse ends at Bürkliplatz, the main departure point for boat trips, with majestic views across the lake to the distant snow-capped mountains. **a** Bahnhofstr. **w** www.bahnhofstrasse-zuerich.ch **N** Tram: 6, 7, 11, 13 (Bahnhofstrasse); Tram: 2, 6, 7, 8, 9, 11, 13 (Paradeplatz); Tram: 2, 8, 9, 11 (Bürkliplatz)

Frauenbadi-Stadthausquai

This small riverside lido is the only surviving example of a typical 19th-century floating lido and it provides an oasis of calm at the heart of the city, open only to women for swimming, massage, yoga and relaxation. By night (from 20.00), it becomes the Barfuss Bar, popular with both men and women, but everyone must be 'barefoot', as the name suggests. ⓐ Stadthausquai ⓣ 044 211 95 92 ⓛ Lido: 07.30–19.30 (mid-May–mid-Sept, depending on water temperature) and from 08.30 at weekends ⓝ Tram: 2, 5, 8, 9, 11 (Bürkliplatz) ⓘ Admission charge

Fraumünster

The main attraction of this elegant church with its slim green spire is the five stained-glass chancel windows created by Marc Chagall in 1970. Each window has its own colour theme; the blue 'Jacob' window, the green 'Christ' window and the yellow 'Zion' window are on the main wall, flanked by the red 'Prophets' window to the left and the blue 'Law' window to the right.

The church itself is situated beside the river, overlooking the picturesque old town square and former pig market, Münsterhof. The edifice dates from the 13th century, built on the site of an early Benedictine abbey, the crypt of which has been preserved beneath the church. ⓐ Fraumünsterstr. ⓦ www.fraumuenster.ch ⓛ 10.00–18.00 Mon–Sat, 11.15–18.00 Sun (Apr–Oct); 10.00–16.00 Mon–Sat, 11.15–16.00 Sun (Nov–Mar) ⓝ Tram: 2, 6, 7, 8, 9, 11, 13 (Paradeplatz)

Limmat (Limmat river)

The city is bisected by the river, which flows from the northern end of Lake Zurich. Its most scenic stretch is from Bahnhofbrücke to Quaibrücke, where the attractive, multicoloured houses of the historic old town flank both banks. Between these two bridges, four further crossing points (Mühlesteg, Rudolf-Brun-Brücke, Rathausbrücke and Münsterbrücke) unite the east and west banks of the city. The Schipfe, Wuhre and Stadthausquai are especially pleasant for strolling. During summer months, cruise vessels ply the river between the Swiss National Museum and the lake.

Lindenhof

The bird's-eye views merit the steep climb to tranquil Lindenhof, the oldest part of Zurich and the original site of the Romans in 15 BC (see page 14). Today this broad, leafy park overlooking the roofs of the Altstadt is an oasis of peace, popular with locals for lunch breaks, and old-timers for *boules* and chess. The surrounding streets contain some of the city's most beautiful medieval wood-framed houses. ⊘ Tram: 6, 7, 11, 13 (Rennweg)

⬤ *The Münsterbrücke links the east and west banks of the Limmat*

St-Peterskirche (St Peter's Church)

No matter where you are in the city, it's hard to miss St Peter's, since it boasts the largest clock face in Europe, 8.7 m (28.5 ft) in diameter. The church itself is the city's oldest parish church, founded in the early 7th century, while the tranquil St Peterhofstatt is considered the Altstadt's loveliest square. ⓐ St Peterhofstatt ⓦ www.st-peter-zh.ch ⓛ 08.00–18.00 Mon–Fri, 08.00–16.00 Sat, closed Sun ⓝ Tram: 6, 7, 11, 13 (Rennweg)

Uetliberg (Uetli Mountain)

Uetliberg is the tallest point in the city, at 871 m (2,857 ft). From here, there is a popular two-hour hiking route along a forested mountain ridge, with glorious views over the city, the lake and the Alps. Just 15 minutes from the high-tech, jet-set glamour of the city centre, you can escape to the lush meadows, tinkling cowbells and chocolate-box landscapes that set Switzerland apart. ⓝ S-Bahn: Uetliberg

Zürichsee (Lake Zurich)

The 'blue lung' of the city and the fourth largest lake in Switzerland is hugely popular with Zürchers for boating, strolling, swimming, sunbathing, barbecuing or simply chilling out. No trip to Zurich is complete without a mini-cruise to admire the grandiose mansions lining the shores, and Bürkliplatz is the chief departure point for boat trips on the lake. Choose from a variety of year-round excursions ranging from nostalgic paddle-steamer tours to fondue cruises (see page 102).

CULTURE

Haus Konstruktiv (House for Constructive Art)

The Constructive Art Movement was founded in Zurich. Leading exponents Max Bill, Verena Loewensberg, Camille Graeser and Richard Paul Lohse all had their ateliers here, and their abstract art forms, based on geometric principles, came to the fore during World War II. Today the Foundation for Constructive Art is housed in a former power station on the Sihl River, close to the city centre, and hosts regular temporary exhibitions to promote Constructivist, Concrete and Concept art and design. ❸ ewz-Unterwerk Selnau, Selnaustr. 25 ❶ 044 217 70 80 ⓦ www.hauskonstruktiv.ch ❶ 12.00–18.00 Tues, Thur & Fri, 12.00–20.00 Wed, 11.00–18.00 Sat & Sun, closed Mon ◎ Tram: 8 (Bahnhof Selnau); Tram: 2, 3, 9, 14 (Stauffacher) ❶ Admission charge

Museum Rietberg

Set in lush parkland, the Rietberg Museum is Switzerland's only gallery for non-European cultures, and boasts an internationally renowned collection of art from Asia, Africa, America and Oceania. The core of the collection was donated to the city by Baron Eduard von der Heydt in 1952. Following a major new extension, which opened in 2007, the museum more than doubled its exhibition space. Highlights of the Buddhist art collections can be seen in the magnificent neoclassical Villa Wesendonck – once home to the 19th-century German composer, with ancient Islamic and Indian paintings and Middle Eastern textiles displayed in Villa Rieter, located in Rieterpark, both named after an industrial family. The Emerald underground extension contains predominantly Chinese art, while the 'Visible Storage' area provides a chance to see museum life behind the scenes.

ⓐ Gablerstr. 15 ⓣ 044 206 31 31 ⓦ www.rietberg.ch
ⓛ 10.00–17.00 Tues–Sun (until 20.00 Wed & Thur), closed Mon
ⓝ Tram: 7 (Museum Rietberg) ⓘ Admission charge

Uhrenmuseum Beyer Zurich (Clock & Watch Museum Beyer Zurich)

This small but fascinating museum in the basement of the celebrated Beyer Chronometrie store contains over 500 time-pieces ranging from wooden-wheel clocks, water clocks, sundials and traditional cuckoo-clocks to state-of-the-art contemporary navigational instruments. The shop sells many famous Swiss brands: Rolex, Cartier, Patek Philippe, Breitling, Jaeger LeCoultre.

ⓐ Bahnhofstr. 31 ⓣ 043 344 63 63 ⓦ www.beyer-ch.com
ⓛ 14.00–18.00 Mon–Fri, closed Sat & Sun ⓝ Tram: 2, 6, 7, 8, 9, 11, 13 (Paradeplatz) ⓘ Admission charge

Zunfthaus zur Meisen (Guildhall zur Meisen)

The Swiss National Museum's exhibition of porcelain and faience includes a fine collection of delicate 18th-century figurines and dishes from the Zurich porcelain factory in Kilchberg-Schooren. The Zunfthaus zur Meisen, one of the city's most beautiful guild houses, richly embellished with stuccos, is a perfect backdrop for the exquisite displays of Baroque table decoration.

ⓐ Münsterhof 20 ⓣ 044 221 28 07 ⓦ www.musee-suisse.ch
ⓛ 10.30–17.00 Tues–Sun, closed Mon ⓝ Tram: 2, 6, 7, 8, 9, 11, 13 (Paradeplatz) ⓘ Admission charge

RETAIL THERAPY

Alprausch A real souvenir alternative to Swiss chocolate, this young, trendy boutique epitomises Swiss design with its urban fashions, snow-wear and accessories. ⓐ Werdmühlepl. 4 ⓣ 043 497 32 00 ⓦ www.alprausch.com ⓛ 10.00–19.00 Mon–Fri, 10.00–17.00 Sat, closed Sun ⓝ Tram: 6, 7, 11, 13 (Bahnhofstrasse)

Bally Capitol The world's largest outlet of this famous Swiss institution. ⓐ Bahnhofstr. 66 ⓣ 044 224 39 39 ⓦ www.bally.com ⓛ 09.30–19.00 Mon–Wed & Fri, 09.30–20.00 Thur, 10.00–18.00 Sat, closed Sun ⓝ Tram: 6, 7, 11, 13 (Bahnhofstrasse)

Bucherer An old favourite for jewellery and watches. Look out for Chopard, Tag Heuer, Rolex and other famous Swiss brands. ⓐ Bahnhofstr. 50 ⓣ 044 211 26 35 ⓦ www.bucherer.com ⓛ 09.00–19.00 Mon–Fri, 09.00–17.00 Sat, closed Sun ⓝ Tram: 6, 7, 11, 13 (Bahnhofstrasse)

Chäs Vreneli A small cheese shop, renowned beyond the Swiss borders for its selection of regional cheeses. Try the Tilsiter, Appenzeller, Emmental or, for fondue, some Gruyère and Vacherin Fribourgeois. ⓐ Münsterhof 7 ⓣ 044 221 32 81 ⓦ www.chaes-vreneli.ch ⓛ 06.30–18.30 Mon–Fri, 06.30–16.00 Sat, closed Sun ⓝ Tram: 2, 6, 7, 8, 9, 11, 13 (Paradeplatz)

Confiserie Sprüngli Sprüngli is Switzerland's most famous chocolatier, founded in 1836. Still today the world-famous *pralinés*, *truffes du jour*, *Luxembourgerli* (tiny, cream-filled, coloured meringues) and other specialities are lovingly handmade daily, following traditional recipes. Upstairs is a coffee shop. ⓐ Bahnhofstr. 21, Am Paradepl. ① 044 224 47 11 ⓦ www.spruengli.ch ⓛ 07.30–18.30 Mon–Fri, 08.00–17.00 Sat, closed Sun ⓝ Tram: 2, 6, 7, 8, 9, 11, 13 (Paradeplatz)

Edo Popken In his small boutique at the heart of the banking district, Swiss designer Edo Popken provides shirts and ties for the best-dressed men in town. ⓐ Bärengasse 10 ① 044 221 25 08 ⓦ www.edopopken.ch ⓛ 09.00–18.30 Mon–Fri (until 20.00 Thur), 09.00–17.00 Sat, closed Sun ⓝ Tram: 2, 6, 7, 8, 9, 11, 13 (Paradeplatz)

Fabric Frontline The exceptional silks here, ranging from ties and scarves to reams of fabric in vivid colours and prints, draw such designers as Lacroix, Givenchy and Vivienne Westwood to this small textile house. ⓐ Ankerstr. 118 ① 044 241 64 55 ⓦ www.fabricfrontline.ch ⓛ 10.00–18.30 Mon–Fri, 10.00–16.00 Sat, closed Sun ⓝ Tram: 8 (Helvetiaplatz)

Franz Carl Weber One of the largest toy shops in Europe and every child's dream, with its impressive window displays and dazzling range of toys for all ages. ⓐ Bahnhofstr. 62 ① 044 225 78 78 ⓦ www.fcw.ch ⓛ 09.00–18.30 Mon–Wed, 09.00–20.00 Thur & Fri, 09.00–1800 Sat, closed Sun ⓝ Tram: 6, 7, 11, 13 (Bahnhofstrasse)

Globus If you can't find it at Globus, you can probably do without it; there are seven floors of fashion, jewellery, toiletries, stationery, and a sensational delicatessen. ⓐ Schweizergasse 11

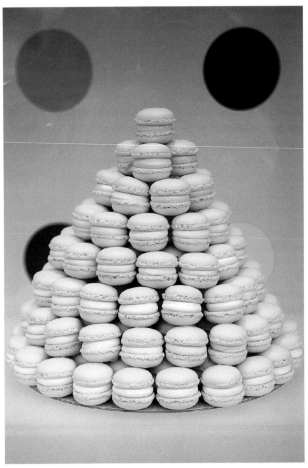

⬤ *If you like meringues, you'll love* Luxembourgerli

🕿 044 226 60 60 Ⓦ www.globus.ch 🕒 09.00–20.00 Mon–Sat, closed Sun Ⓝ Tram: 6, 7, 11, 13 (Bahnhofstrasse)

Grieder This spacious, sophisticated store specialises in prêt-a-porter, haute-couture and exclusive accessories for men and women by such designers as Armani, Kenzo, Gaultier, Fendi and Choo. Ⓐ Bahnhofstr. 30 🕿 044 224 36 36 Ⓦ www.bongenie-grieder.ch 🕒 09.00–19.00 Mon–Fri, 09.30–18.00 Sat, closed Sun Ⓝ Tram: 2, 6, 7, 8, 9, 11, 13 (Paradeplatz)

Jelmoli Zurich's largest and most popular department store. Ⓐ Seidengasse 1 🕿 044 220 44 11 Ⓦ www.jelmoli.ch 🕒 09.00–20.00 Mon–Sat, closed Sun Ⓝ Tram: 6, 7, 11, 13 (Rennweg)

Pastorini Spielzeug A magical toy shop, with three floors of imaginative wooden toys, musical instruments, dolls and puppets, crafts and educational games. Ⓐ Weinpl. 3 🕿 044 228 70 70 Ⓦ www.pastorini.ch 🕒 13.30–18.30 Mon, 09.30–18.30 Tues–Fri, 09.30–17.00 Sat, closed Sun Ⓝ Tram: 6, 7, 11, 13 (Rennweg)

Schweizer Heimatwerk *The* shop for top-quality contemporary Swiss craftwork, with everything from ceramic kitchenware and glass to jewellery and clothing, woodwork and toys. Ⓐ Uraniastr. 1 🕿 044 222 19 55 Ⓦ www.heimatwerk.ch 🕒 09.00–20.00 Mon–Fri, 09.00–18.00 Sat, closed Sun Ⓝ Tram: 4, 15 (Rudolf-Brun-Brücke)

Sibler This wonderful design shop is brimming with witty yet practical household items and gift ideas. From Buddah-shaped jelly moulds to contraptions that cleanly take off the tip of your boiled egg, you can find it here. ⓐ Münsterhof 16 ⓣ 044 211 55 50 ⓦ www.sibler-shop.ch ⓛ 10.00–19.00 Mon–Fri, 09.00–18.30 Sat, closed Sun Ⓝ Tram: 2, 6, 7, 8, 9, 11, 13 (Paradeplatz)

Spitzenhaus Labor An old-fashioned shop, filled with fine table linens from Bern and Zurich and lace from St Gallen and Appenzell. ⓐ Börsenstr. 14 ⓣ 044 211 55 76 ⓛ 09.30–12.30, 13.30–18.30 Mon–Fri, 09.30–16.30 Sat, closed Sun Ⓝ Tram: 2, 8, 9, 11 (Bürkliplatz)

Swatch First launched in 1983, the simple, plastic Swiss-designed Swatch is the most successful wrist-watch of all time. Check out the latest seasonal collections here. ⓐ Bahnhofstr. 94 ⓣ 044 221 28 66 ⓦ www.swatch.ch ⓛ 09.30–19.00 Mon–Fri, 09.00–17.00 Sat, closed Sun Ⓝ Tram: 6, 7, 11, 13 (Bahnhofstrasse)

Teuscher This elaborately decorated Altstadt chocolate shop tempts passers-by to stop for a box of speciality handmade truffles. Try the champagne and orange ones! ⓐ Storchengasse 9 ⓣ 044 211 51 53 ⓦ www.teuscher.com ⓛ 08.00–18.30 Mon–Fri, 08.00–17.00 Sat, 16.00–18.00 Sun Ⓝ Tram: 2, 6, 7, 8, 9, 11, 13 (Paradeplatz)

TAKING A BREAK

Confiserie Sprüngli £ ❶ The most select café in town, overlooking Paradeplatz, full of old-time Zürchers enjoying fine

cakes, chocolates and pâtisserie. ⓐ Bahnhofstr. 21, Am Paradepl.
ⓣ 044 224 47 11 ⓦ www.confiserie-spruengli.ch
ⓛ 07.30–18.30 Mon–Fri, 08.00–17.00 Sat, closed Sun ⓝ Tram: 2, 6,
7, 8, 9, 11, 13 (Paradeplatz)

Mishio £–££ ❷ Trendy, minimalist noodle bar serving tasty pan-
Asian cuisine to eat in or take away. ⓐ Sihlstr. 9 ⓣ 044 228 76 76
ⓦ www.mishio.ch ⓛ 06.30–23.00 Mon–Sat, closed Sun
ⓝ Tram: 6, 7, 11, 13 (Rennweg)

Bona Dea ££ ❸ This vegetarian buffet restaurant beside the
Hauptbahnhof offers a wide choice of delicious salads and
Asian-influenced dishes, with fresh juices and even organic
beers and wines. ⓐ Bahnhofpl. 15 ⓣ 044 217 15 15
ⓦ www.bona-dea.ch ⓛ 11.30–14.30, 17.30–23.00 daily
ⓝ Tram: 3, 4, 6, 7, 10, 11, 13, 14 (Bahnhofplatz)

Grieder ££ ❹ A favourite haunt for well-heeled shoppers. Enjoy
a coffee or a light lunch on the tree-shaded rooftop terrace.
ⓐ Bahnhofstr. 30 ⓣ 044 224 36 36 ⓦ www.bongenie-grieder.ch
ⓛ 09.30–19.00 Mon–Fri, 09.30–18.00 Sat, closed Sun
ⓝ Tram: 2, 6, 7, 8, 9, 11, 13 (Paradeplatz)

Hiltl ££ ❺ Hiltl was Europe's first vegetarian eatery when it
opened in 1898. Today it remains Zurich's top vegetarian restaurant
with an excellent salad bar and superb curries, too. ⓐ Sihlstr. 28
ⓣ 044 227 70 00 ⓦ www.hiltl.ch ⓛ 06.00–24.00 Mon–Wed,
06.00–04.00 Thur–Sat, 08.00–24.00 Sun ⓝ Tram: 2, 6, 7, 8, 9, 11,
13 (Paradeplatz)

AFTER DARK

RESTAURANTS

Reithalle £ ❻ The former military riding school has been converted into a bar, restaurant, theatre and centre of performing arts. Enjoy a variety of tasty, international dishes. ⓐ Gessnerallee 8 ⓣ 044 212 70 66 ⓦ www.restaurant-reithalle.ch ⓛ 11.00–24.00 Mon–Fri, 18.00–24.00 Sat, 18.00–23.00 Sun ⓝ Tram: 3 (Kaserne)

Zeughauskeller £ ❼ A converted 15th-century arsenal, now the city's top beer hall, serves traditional Swiss cuisine alongside steins of local beer. The metre-long sausage feeds four. ⓐ Bahnhofstr. 28A ⓣ 044 211 26 90 ⓦ www.zeughauskeller.ch ⓛ 11.30–23.00 daily ⓝ Tram: 2, 6, 7, 8, 9, 11, 13 (Paradeplatz)

Zum Kropf £ ❽ The 'Kropf' serves hearty portions of traditional Zurich cuisine and fine beers in a Bavarian-style beer hall. ⓐ In Gassen 16 ⓣ 044 221 18 05 ⓦ www.zumkropf.ch ⓛ 11.30–23.30 Mon–Sat, closed Sun ⓝ Tram: 2, 6, 7, 8, 9, 11, 13 (Paradeplatz)

Contrapunto ££ ❾ Linger over a meal on the pavement terrace at this elegant modern Italian restaurant. ⓐ Waaggasse 5/7 ⓣ 044 211 65 25 ⓛ 11.30–23.30 Mon–Sat, 11.30–22.00 Sun ⓝ Tram: 2, 6, 7, 8, 9, 11, 13 (Paradeplatz)

Tao's ££–£££ ❿ Enjoy delicious Euro-Asian cuisine in this sophisticated, modern-oriental restaurant-cum-lounge bar. ⓐ Augustinergasse 3 ⓣ 044 448 11 22 ⓦ www.taos-lounge.ch ⓛ 12.00–01.00 Mon–Sat, closed Sun ⓝ Tram: 6, 7, 11, 13 (Rennweg)

Caduff's Wine Loft £££ ⓫ This stylish restaurant boasts more than 2,500 different wines, a tempting Mediterranean menu and the longest bar in town. ⓐ Kanzleistr. 126 ⓣ 044 240 22 55 ⓦ www.wineloft.ch ⓛ 11.00–14.30, 17.00–24.00 Mon–Fri, 17.00–24.00 Sat ⓝ Tram: 2, 3 (Kalkbreite); Tram: 8 (Bäckeranlage)

Segantini £££ ⓬ This upmarket restaurant and beautiful garden terrace draws a media and fashion crowd. ⓐ Ankerstr. 120 ⓣ 044 241 07 00 ⓦ www.segantini.ch ⓛ 11.00–14.00, 18.00–24.00 Tues–Fri, 18.00–24.00 Sat ⓝ Tram: 8 (Helvetiaplatz)

Zunfthaus zur Waag £££ ⓭ Top-notch Swiss cuisine within a beautiful 17th-century guild house. ⓐ Münsterhof 8 ⓣ 044 216 99 66 ⓦ www.zunfthaus-zur-waag.ch ⓛ 11.30–14.00, 18.00–22.00 daily ⓝ Tram: 2, 6, 7, 8, 9, 11, 13 (Paradeplatz)

BARS & CLUBS

Jules Verne Panoramabar Enjoy dazzling 360° views of Zürich by night in this trendy panoramic wine bar. ⓐ Uraniastr. 9 ⓣ 044 888 66 66 ⓦ www.jules-verne.ch ⓝ Tram: 6, 7, 11, 13 (Rennweg)

Kaufleuten Rub shoulders with celebrities at one of the most glamorous nightclubs in town. ⓐ Pelikanstr. 18 ⓣ 044 225 33 22 ⓦ www.kaufleuten.com ⓝ Tram: 6, 7, 11, 13 (Rennweg)

Widder A cosy piano bar with over 800 spirits and top-notch live jazz most weeks. ⓐ Rennweg 7 ⓣ 044 224 25 26 ⓦ www.widderhotel.ch ⓝ Tram: 6, 7, 11, 13 (Rennweg)

Niederdorf & beyond

The picturesque Niederdorf district, on the right bank of the Limmat, forms the eastern half of the city's Altstadt and provides a perfect counterpart to glitzy, glamorous Central Zurich on the left bank, with its chic shopping streets and finance houses. Niederdorf has a special, village-like charm with its hilly, cobbled lanes, medieval houses painted in pastel shades and historic guildhalls. Its centrepiece is the Grossmünster, a veritable city landmark with its enormous twin towers. Above the Altstadt is the university with its grandiose architecture, and Switzerland's top gallery, the Kunsthaus. To the south there is a wonderful lakeside walk to Zürichhorn Park, past lidos, boat hire, cafés, museums and ornamental gardens.

SIGHTS & ATTRACTIONS

Botanischer Garten der Universität Zürich (Botanic Garden of Zurich University)

The stunning plant collections here provide a botanical world tour, from alpine roses and Mediterranean herbs to desert plants and tropical rainforests. Over 9,000 different types of plants grow on 53,000 sq m (570,487 sq ft), while the grand lawn and pond make good resting spots from which to admire the garden. ⓐ Zollikerstr. 107 ⓣ 044 634 8461 ⓦ www.bguz.uzh.ch ⓛ Garden: 07.00–19.00 Mon–Fri, 08.00–18.00 Sat & Sun (Mar–Sept); 08.00–18.00 Mon–Fri, 07.00–17.00 Sat & Sun (Oct–Feb); greenhouses: 09.30–16.00 (17.00 during summer weekends) ⓝ Bus: 33, 77 (Botanischer Garten)

HEADLESS SAINTS!

Zurich's cathedral is dedicated to the city's patron saints, Felix, Regula and Exuperantius, who attempted to convert its citizens to Christianity in the 3rd century. According to legend, the governor of the city made them drink molten lead and plunged them into boiling oil. They still refused to renounce their faith, so they were beheaded. Miraculously, even this didn't stop them. They picked up their heads, carried them to the top of a hill (where the cathedral stands today), dug their own graves and then buried themselves. Zurich's seal still honours these martyrs, portrayed carrying their heads under their arms. Their remains are kept in one of the Grossmünster's chapels.

Chinagarten Zürich (Zurich China Garden)

This lovely traditional South China garden was a gift from Zurich's twin town, Kunming. Dedicated to 'the three winter friends' (pine, bamboo and winter cherry), and with ponds, pagodas, exotic planting and inscriptions and paintings, it is an oasis of calm at Zürichhorn Park. ⓐ Bellerivestr. ⓣ 044 380 31 51 ⓦ www.chinagarten.ch ⓛ 11.00–19.00 daily (late Mar–late Oct) ⓝ Bus: 912, 916 (Chinagarten) ⓘ Admission charge

Grossmünster (Cathedral)

This imposing Romanesque and Gothic cathedral with its two mighty towers stands proudly on a terrace overlooking the Limmat River. According to legend, it was founded by

Charlemagne, whose horse faltered at the graves of three early Christian martyrs, Zurich's patron saints, Felix and Regula, and their servant, Exuperantius.

In the early 16th century, it was the parish church of Huldrych Zwingli and the birthplace of the Reformation (see page 14). In accordance with Zwingli's beliefs, the interior of the Grossmünster is austere. The choir contains stained-glass windows by Augusto Giacometti, which depict the Christmas story, and there is a Renaissance statue of Charlemagne in the crypt. The bird's-eye views from the top of the tower merit the 187-step climb.
ⓐ Grossmünsterpl. ☎ 044 252 59 49 ⓦ www.grossmuenster.ch
🕙 10.00–18.00 daily (Mar–Oct); 10.00–17.00 daily (Nov–Feb)
Ⓝ Tram: 4 ❶ Admission charge for tower

Niederdorf

The eastern part of Zurich's Altstadt is centred on the Niederdorf, a predominantly car-free, village-like district known to locals as the 'Dörfli', which stretches southwards along the riverside for about a kilometre. With its cobbled alleyways awash with small cafés, bars and boutiques, and its sunny courtyards splashed with medieval fountains, it is one of Zurich's most popular districts. During summer months on Niederdorfstrasse (the main street), the cafés and restaurants spill out on to pavement terraces to create a lively atmosphere. Ⓝ Tram: 4, 15 (Rathaus or Helmhaus); Tram: 3, 4, 6, 7, 10, 15 (Central); Tram: 3 (Neumarkt)

Seebad Utoquai

Join sun-seekers at this popular lakeside lido, with a smart sun-terrace, bar, restaurant, sauna and massage facilities, and boat hire.

ⓐ Utoquai ⓣ 044 251 61 51 ⓛ 07.00–20.00 daily (mid-May–late Sept) Ⓝ Tram: 2, 4 (Kreuzstrasse) ⓘ Admission charge

Zoo Zurich

The city zoo is more than just an animal park. It focuses on endangered animals and attempts to provide authentic habitats for its more than 360 species of animals from around the globe. It has even re-created a Masoala rainforest in its midst. Young children love the Zoolino petting area. ⓐ Zürichbergstr. 221 ⓣ 044 254 25 05 Ⓦ www.zoo.ch ⓛ 09.00–18.00 daily (Mar–Oct) (Masoala rainforest from 10.00); 09.00–17.00 daily (Nov–Feb) (Masoala rainforest from 10.00) Ⓝ Tram: 6 (Zoo) ⓘ Admission charge

● *A typical narrow, cobbled lane, Niederdorf*

Zürichsee (Lake Zurich)

One of the city's most pleasurable experiences is to stroll along the east bank of the lake, admire its beautiful scenery by day and by night, and enjoy its many facilities, which range from pedalo hire to steamboat excursions, restaurants, lidos, picnic areas, gardens and even an open-air cinema in summer. Look out for the attractive **Museum Bellerive**, with its changing exhibitions of applied arts (ⓐ Höschgasse 3 ⓦ www.museum-bellerive.ch ⓘ Admission charge); the Chinagarten and Jean Tinguely's perpetual-motion sculpture *Heureka*, built for the 1964 National Exhibition. Take a break at one of the cafés or enjoy fresh fish at the Fischstube at Zürichhorn.

CULTURE

Cabaret Voltaire

The Dada art movement was founded here at Cabaret Voltaire almost a hundred years ago in 1916, and was a popular rendezvous for such artists and writers as Hans Arp and Hugo Ball (see page 12). Today it contains a small museum devoted to Dadaism and an arty café. ⓐ Spiegelgasse 1 ⓣ 043 268 57 20 ⓦ www.cabaretvoltaire.ch ⓛ Museum: 12.30–18.30 Tues–Fri & Sat, 11.00–19.00 Sun, closed Mon. Café: 12.00–24.00 Tues–Sat, 12.30–18.30 Sun, closed Mon ⓝ Tram: 4, 15 (Rathaus) ⓘ Admission charge

E G Bührle Collection

One of the world's most celebrated private art collections, housed in an elegant 19th-century villa. Industrialist Emil

Bührle's paintings include some major old master works, but the focal point is his dazzling French Impressionist collection, with significant works by such artists as Cézanne, Monet, Picasso, Renoir and Van Gogh. Since the big robbery here in early 2008, opening times have been restricted. It is currently open on the first Sunday of each month for individual visitors and for groups on request. Check the website for the latest info.
🅐 Zollikerstr. 172 🕐 044 422 00 86 🆆 www.buehrle.ch
Ⓝ Tram: 2, 4 (Wildbachstrasse) ❶ Admission charge

Heidi-Weber-Haus, Centre Le Corbusier

'A house is a machine for living in' once remarked the celebrated Swiss architect and visual artist Le Corbusier. He created the Heidi-Weber-Haus to represent the culmination of his studies in the fields of architecture, interior design and visual arts, and to serve as a museum of his life and works. The resulting minimalist edifice of glass and steel, with its brightly coloured enamel blocks and umbrella roof, was his last building, completed posthumously in 1967, and reflects his ideological formalism. 🅐 Höschgasse 8 🕐 044 383 64 70 🆆 www.lecorbusier-center.com 🕐 14.00–17.00 Sat & Sun, closed Mon–Fri (July–Sept) Ⓝ Bus: 912, 916 (Chinagarten) ❶ Admission charge

Helmhaus & Wasserkirche (Water Church)

According to legend, the gothic Water Church was constructed on the execution site of Felix and Regula, Zurich's patron saints (see page 77). Like the city's other churches, it was robbed of its treasures during the Reformation. The adjacent Baroque Helmhaus has been used as a courtroom and a covered market

over the years. Today it is an imaginative exhibition space
for young artists to showcase contemporary Swiss art.
🅐 Limmatquai 31 🅣 044 251 61 77 🅦 www.helmhaus.org
🅛 10.00–18.00 Tues–Sun, closed Mon 🅝 Tram: 4, 15 (Helmhaus)

Kunsthaus (Museum of Fine Arts)

The collections in Switzerland's premier art gallery span Swiss
and international art from the Middle Ages to the present day,
and contain major loans of Impressionist and Expressionist
works. The museum's audio guides provide in-depth
information on over 200 artworks by all the big names,
including Rembrandt, Rubens, Tiepolo, Monet, Picasso, Rodin,
Dalí, Lichtenstein and Pollock. Highlights include paintings
by Zürcher Post-Reformation artists, 19th- and 20th-century
Swiss art, the Edvard Munch collection (the largest outside
Oslo), and the Swiss-born Alberto Giacometti Foundation.
🅐 Heimpl. 1 🅣 044 253 84 84 🅦 www.kunsthaus.ch 🅛 10.00–18.00
Sat, Sun & Tues, 10.00–20.00 Wed–Fri, closed Mon
🅝 Tram: 3, 5, 8, 9 (Kunsthaus) 🅘 Admission charge

Opernhaus (Opera house)

This imposing edifice counts among Europe's leading opera
houses, built in 1890 in the late Baroque style and famous for
its world-class productions. 🅐 Falkenstr. 1 🅣 044 268 64 00
🅦 www.opernhaus.ch 🅝 Tram: 2, 4 (Opernhaus)

Universität (University)

Zürich boasts Switzerland's leading university, the Federal
Institute of Technology (ETH), which, over the years, has

produced 28 Nobel Prize winners, including Albert Einstein, who especially enjoyed the city views from the Polyterrace, which is open to visitors. The university complex contains a rich selection of highly specialised museums, including the **Archäologische Sammlung der Universität** (Archaeological Collection ⓦ www.archinst.uhz.ch), the **Graphisches Sammlung der ETH** (Collection of Prints and Drawings ⓦ www.graphischesammlung.ch), the **Thomas-Mann-Archiv der ETH** (Thomas Mann Archive ⓦ www.tma.ethz.ch), the **Paläontologisches Museum** (Paleontology Museum ⓦ www.pim.uzh.ch), the **Medizinhistorisches Museum der Universität** (Museum of the History of Medicine ⓦ www.medizin-museum.uzh.ch) and the **Zoologisches Museum der Universität** (Zoological Museum ⓦ www.zm.uzh.ch). ⓐ Rämistr. 71 ⓣ 044 635 44 01 Ⓣ Tram: 6, 9, 10 (ETH/Universitätsspital)

⬤ *The Chinagarten Zürich is an oasis of calm (see page 77)*

RETAIL THERAPY

Musik Hug A top-notch store for Swiss folkloric music, jazz and classical recordings. ⓐ Limmatquai 28–30 ① 044 269 41 41 ⓦ www.musikhug.ch ⓛ 09.00–18.30 Mon–Fri, 09.00–17.00 Sat, closed Sun ⓝ Tram: 4, 15 (Helmhaus)

Neumarkt 17 One of the most extraordinary shops in Zurich, this is a rabbit warren of stylish interior design and modern furnishing. ⓐ Neumarkt 17 ① 044 254 38 38 ⓦ www.neumarkt17.ch ⓛ 09.00–18.30 Tues–Fri, 09.00–17.00 Sat, closed Sun & Mon ⓝ Tram: 3 (Neumarkt)

⬤ *Schwarzenbach, an old-fashioned Niederdorf grocery shop*

Schwarzenbach An old-fashioned grocery shop in Niederdorf specialising in 'colonial goods', including teas, coffees, nuts, dried fruit, herbs and spices, oils and chocolates. There is a small café, too. ⓐ Münstergasse 19 ⓣ 044 261 13 15 ⓦ www.schwarzenbach.ch ⓛ 08.00–18.30 Tues–Fri, 09.00–17.00 Sat, closed Sun & Mon ⓝ Tram: 4, 15 (Rathaus)

Stefi Talman The unique shoes, boots, bags and accessories of this Swiss-born designer are contemporary, comfortable and stylish. ⓐ Oberdorfstrasse 13 ⓣ 044 252 81 10 ⓛ 12.00–18.30 Mon, 10.00–18.30 Tues–Fri, 10.00–17.00 Sat, closed Sun ⓝ Tram: 2, 4, 5, 8, 9, 15 (Bellevue)

Travel Book Shop A treasure trove of maps and travel books from all over the world, many in English. A must for globetrotters! ⓐ Rindermarkt 20 ⓣ 044 252 38 83 ⓦ www.travelbookshop.ch ⓛ 09.00–18.30 Tues–Fri, 09.00–17.00 Sat, closed Sun & Mon ⓝ Tram: 4, 5 (Rathaus)

TAKING A BREAK

Altstadt £ ❶ This cool café-bar near the Grossmünster is a popular meeting point for breakfast, coffee, lunch or a relaxed aperitif. ⓐ Kirchgasse 4 ⓣ 044 250 53 53 ⓦ www.hotel-altstadt.ch ⓛ 07.00–24.00 daily ⓝ Tram: 4, 15 (Helmhaus)

Café Schober £ ❷ A delightful old-fashioned tearoom and Zürich's oldest confectionery, serving delicious coffees, hot chocolate with whipped cream, mouthwatering pastries and

chocolates. ⓐ Napfgasse 4 ❶ 044 251 80 60 ⓦ www.cafe-
conditorei-schober.ch ● 08.00–19.00 Mon–Wed, 08.00–23.00
Thur–Sat, 09.00–19.00 Sun Ⓝ Tram: 4, 15 (Rathaus)

Café Zähringer £ ❸ Popular with students, this bright,
atmospheric café serves healthy, organic food, with a good daily
vegetarian selection. ⓐ Zähringerpl. 11 ❶ 044 252 05 00
ⓦ www.cafe-zaehringer.ch ● 09.00–24.00 Tues–Sun,
18.00–24.00 Mon Ⓝ Tram: 4, 15 (Rudolf-Brun-Brücke)

Mövenpick Ice Cream Gallery £ ❹ Treat yourself to a Swiss-
made ice cream, by the lake, in a bewildering choice of
flavours, including espresso, pistachio, grapefruit, apple,
Swiss chocolate. ⓐ Theaterstr. 8 ❶ 043 268 04 20
ⓦ www.moevenpick-icecream.com ● 11.00–23.00 daily
Ⓝ Tram: 2, 4, 5, 8, 9, 11, 15 (Bellevue)

Sternen Grill £ ❺ This sausage stand serves the best fast
food in town. Even local resident Tina Turner queues here
for a 'St Galler Bratwurst mit Gold Burli' (a sausage wrapped
in paper, a bowl of mustard to dunk it in and a crusty roll).
ⓐ Bellevuepl. ❶ 044 251 49 49 ● 10.30–24.00 daily (until 01.00
Fri & Sat) Ⓝ Tram: 2, 4, 5, 8, 9, 11, 15 (Bellevue)

Globus Am Bellevue ££ ❻ Eat your way around the world
with light bites and takeaway tapas, panini, noodles, curries
and sushi. ⓐ Theaterstr. 12 ❶ 044 266 16 16 ⓦ www.globus.ch
● 07.00–23.30 Mon–Thur, 07.00–24.00 Fri, 08.00–24.00 Sat,
10.00–22.00 Sun Ⓝ Tram: 2, 4, 5, 8, 9, 11, 15 (Bellevue)

Tibits by Hiltl ££ ❼ Vegetarian fast food for fashionable, health-conscious Zürchers. Try the sensational buffet. ⓐ Seefeldstr. 2 ☏ 044 260 32 22 ⓦ www.tibits.ch ⏱ 06.30–24.00 Mon–Fri, 08.00–24.00 Sat, 09.00–24.00 Sun ⓝ Tram: 2, 4 (Opernhaus)

AFTER DARK

RESTAURANTS

Crazy Cow £ ❽ Hearty Swiss cuisine in a witty restaurant. The menu is in Swiss dialect (with English translations). Try the scrumptuous *rösti* dishes or the Alpen Macaroni. ⓐ Leonhardstr. 1 ☏ 044 261 40 55 ⓦ www.crazycow.ch ⏱ 11.00–23.00 daily ⓝ Tram: 6, 7, 10, 15 (Haldenegg)

Adler's Swiss Chuchi £–££ ❾ Excellent-value fondues and *raclette* dishes in a bright, modern, alpine setting, plus plenty of authentic Swiss specialities for non-cheese-lovers. ⓐ Rosengasse 10 ☏ 044 266 96 96 ⓦ www.hotel-adler.ch ⏱ 11.30–23.15 daily ⓝ Tram: 4, 15 (Rudolf-Brun-Brücke)

Blinde Kuh £–££ ❿ As the world's first 'dark restaurant', the hugely popular Blinde Kuh ('Blind Man's Bluff') offers the unique experience of losing your sight for the duration of your meal as you dine in total darkness. ⓐ Mühlebachstr. 148 ☏ 044 421 50 50 ⓦ www.blindekuh.ch ⏱ 18.30–23.00 Tues–Sat, 18.00–23.00 Sun, closed Mon ⓝ Tram: 2, 4 (Höschgasse) ❶ Reservation essential

Bodega Espanola ££ ⓫ This cosy, rustic, first-floor restaurant serves traditional Spanish fare. On the ground floor is a buzzing tapas bar.

ⓐ Münstergasse 15 ❶ 044 251 23 10 ⏰ Restaurant: 12.00–14.00, 18.00–24.00; tapas bar: 10.00–24.00 daily Ⓝ Tram: 4, 15 (Rathaus)

Le Dezaley ££ ⓬ A friendly restaurant specialising in traditional Vaudois dishes, including superb fondues, served in a series of characterful dining rooms. ⓐ Römergasse 7, off Limmatquai ❶ 044 251 61 29 Ⓦ www.le-dezaley.ch ⏰ 11.30–14.00, 18.00–24.00 Mon–Sat, closed Sun Ⓝ Tram: 4, 15 (Helmhaus)

Mère Catherine ££ ⓭ Enjoy Provençal cuisine at this small courtyard restaurant in the heart of Niederdorf. ⓐ Nägelihof 3, off Limmatquai ❶ 044 250 59 40 Ⓦ www.commercio.ch ⏰ 11.30–14.00, 17.45–24.00 Mon–Fri, 11.30–24.00 Sat & Sun Ⓝ Tram: 4, 15 (Rathaus)

Blaue Ente £££ ⓮ Join Zurich's smart set for light and sophisticated French cooking. At night the restaurant's lounge converts into a fashionable chill-out bar. ⓐ Seefeldstr. 223 ❶ 044 388 68 40 Ⓦ www.blaue-ente.ch ⏰ 11.30–14.00, 18.00–23.30 Mon–Sat, closed Sun Ⓝ Tram: 2, 4 (Wildbachstrasse)

Haus zum Rüden £££ ⓯ Rich, hearty Swiss cuisine in a stunning Gothic riverside guildhall. ⓐ Limmatquai 42 ❶ 044 261 95 66 Ⓦ www.hauszumrueden.ch ⏰ 12.00–15.00, 18.30–24.00 Mon–Fri, closed Sat & Sun Ⓝ Tram: 4, 15 (Rathaus)

Kronenhalle £££ ⓰ Enjoy upmarket Swiss staples in a traditional setting, with wood-panelled walls adorned with original canvases by such luminaries as Picasso and Chagall.

Rämistr. 4 ☎ 044 262 99 00 🌐 www.kronenhalle.com
🕐 12.00–24.00 daily 🚊 Tram: 2, 4, 5, 8, 9, 11, 15 (Bellevue)

Zunfthaus zur Schmiden £££ 🔟 A classy setting for fine Swiss-German specialities. Try the delicious *Zürcher Geschnetzeltes*.
📍 Marktgasse 20 ☎ 044 250 58 48 🌐 www.zunfthausschmiden.ch
🕐 11.30–14.30, 18.00–23.30 Tues–Fri 🚊 Tram: 4, 15 (Rathaus)

BARS & CLUBS

Ba Ba Lu This trendy postmodern bar in Niederdorf, complete with DJ and live music, attracts a young, lively crowd. 📍 Schmidgasse 6
☎ 044 251 97 32 🚊 Tram: 4, 15 (Rudolf-Brun-Brücke)

Bierhalle Wolf An authentic Germanic-style beer cellar with live oom-pah music nightly. 📍 Limmatquai 132 ☎ 044 251 01 30
🌐 www.bierhalle-wolf.ch 🚊 Tram: 3, 4, 6, 7, 10, 15 (Central)

Mascotte One of the oldest clubs in Switzerland. Parties range from hiphop to rock. 📍 Theaterstr. 10 ☎ 044 260 15 80
🌐 www.mascotte.ch 🚊 Tram: 2, 4, 5, 8, 9, 11, 15 (Bellevue)

Odeon A popular gay haunt, the bar made history in 1912 as a bohemian café-bar frequented by Lenin. 📍 Limmatquai 2 ☎ 044 251 16 50 🌐 www.odeon.ch 🚊 Tram: 2, 4, 5, 8, 9, 11, 15 (Bellevue)

Wein Schenken Wine bar with an impressive list of Swiss and international wines. 📍 Hirschengasse 6 ☎ 043 268 33 33
🌐 www.hirschen-zuerich.ch 🕐 16.30–00.30 Mon–Sat, closed Sun
🚊 Tram: 4, 15 (Rudolf-Brun-Brücke)

Zurich West

The city's former industrial quarter has undergone radical change in the past decade, most noticeably in the once-seedy 'Kreis 5' district around the site of the former Löwenbräu Brewery. It is now the heart of the city's hip scene, a multicultural area brimming with trendy bars, restaurants and clubs, and around-the-clock activity. The area is also notable for its inspirational architectural projects, with several old factories converted into living, office and leisure spaces. Shops, galleries and museums – including the Migros Museum and the Zurich Design Museum – focus on the latest trends in contemporary art, while the more traditional Swiss National Museum is among the nation's top museums.

SIGHTS & ATTRACTIONS

Flussbad Obere Letten

One of the trendiest and most popular lidos, where people come for a dip in the canal or a drift downstream in the river, past sundecks, *boules* and beach volleyball pitches. By night, the right bank of the canal turns into Pier West, an open-air bar with live DJs playing groovy sounds. ⓐ Lettensteg 10 ⓦ www.pierwest.ch ⓣ 044 362 92 00 ⓛ 09.00–20.00 daily (mid-May–mid-Sept) ⓝ Tram: 4, 13 (Limmatplatz)

Platzspitz

During the 1980s, this spacious park behind the Swiss National Museum was sadly known as 'Needle Park', the largest meeting place for drug addicts in Switzerland, and generally avoided by city dwellers. In 1993, the area was smartened up and it is now a popular and tranquil grassy retreat stretching along the rivers Limmat and Sihl. It also marks the starting point for river cruises to the lake. Tram: 4, 11, 13, 14 (Bahnhofquai)

Puls 5

Puls 5 is a trendy lifestyle complex recently constructed at the heart of the former industrial district of Zurich West, beside the Schiffbau. This architecturally innovative development contains at its heart a concrete-wrapped former *Giessereihalle* (foundry), together with a supermarket, fitness centre, apartments, shops, bars and restaurants. Still in its infancy, Puls 5 is fast becoming

⬤ Stained glass at the Schweizerisches Landesmuseum

Zurich West

0 ——— 250 metres
0 ——— 250 yards

Zurich ✈

Limmat

HARDTURM STRASSE

FÖRRLIBUCK STRASSE

DUTTWEILER STR

HARDSTRASSE

INDUSTRIE QUARTIER

ESCHER-WYSS PLATZ

ZOLLY STR

Händelschule

TECHNOPARK STR

SCHIFFBAUSTRASSE

Schiffbau

Kunsthalle Zurich & Migros Museum für Gegenwartskunst

PFINGSTWEIDSTRASSE

❻

❷

HEINRICHSTRASSE

N

DUTTWEILER BRÜCKE

Puls 5

TURBINEN STR

MASCHINEN STR

ZAHNRAD

JOSEF STR

NEUE HARD

VIADUKT STR

GEROLDSTR

NEU GASSE

HOHL STRASSE

HARDBRÜCKE

Hardbrücke Bahnhof

EICHBÜHL STRASSE

Güterbahnhof

KORUSTE

BULLINGER STRASSE

HARDSTRASSE

HOHL

STRASSE

SIHLFELD

ERNA STR

ELMISEN STR

STRASSE

BULLINGER PLATZ

STAUFFACHER

AUSSERSIHL

STRASSE

STRASSE

BADENER

AGNES

ZYPRESSEN STRASSE

KOCH STR

KANZLEI

SEEBAHN

HERM GRÜLLICH STR

STR

STRASSE

HARDAU STR

FRIEDAU STR

DENZLER STR

STRASSE

STRASSE

ERISMANN STR

ANWAND STR

KANZLEISTRE

PFLANSCHUL

FELD

STRASSE

one of the hippest addresses in town. **ⓐ** Puls 5, Turbinenpl.
Ⓦ www.puls5.ch **Ⓝ** Tram: 4, 13 (Escher-Wyss-Platz)

Schiffbau

This striking 19th-century industrial building was once used
for building ships and lake-cruisers. Today the ramshackle red-
brick factory forms the heart of an avant-garde arts complex,
containing a top-notch restaurant, a bar, Zurich's top jazz club,
and a second stage for Zurich's best-known theatre, the
Schauspielhaus. **ⓐ** Schiffbaustr. 4 (off Hardstr.) **Ⓝ** Tram: 4, 13
(Escher-Wyss-Platz)

CULTURE

Kunsthalle Zurich

One of two major museums in the converted Löwenbräu Brewery,
the Kunsthalle focuses on the city's contemporary art scene with
frequently changing exhibitions to showcase the work of up-and-
coming internationally significant new artists. **ⓐ** Limmatstr. 270
(second floor) **ⓘ** 044 272 15 15 **Ⓦ** www.kunsthallezurich.ch
Ⓛ 12.00–18.00 Tues, Wed & Fri, 12.00–20.00 Thur, 11.00–17.00
Sat & Sun, closed Mon **Ⓝ** Tram: 4, 13 (Dammweg) **ⓘ** Admission
charge (free Thur 17.00–20.00)

Migros Museum für Gegenwartskunst (Migros Museum for Contemporary Art)

The permanent collection here contains around 1,300 artworks
by 700 international artists, which rotate on display alongside
changing exhibitions – currently in a temporary location until

2012 when the museum will return to the lofty rooms of the former Löwenbräu Brewery at Limmatstrasse 270.

🅐 Albisreiderstr. 199A ☎ 044 277 20 50
🅦 www.migrosmuseum.ch 🕐 12.00–18.00 Tues, Wed & Fri, 12.00–20.00 Thur, 11.00–17.00 Sat & Sun, closed Mon 🚊 Tram: 3 (Hubertus) ℹ Admission charge

Museum für Gestaltung Zurich (Zurich Design Museum)

This top-notch museum features changing exhibitions on various aspects of design, architecture, photography, visual communications and multimedia, covering everything from 'Swiss-made' consumer goods to 'Gay Chic' and 'Takeaway' (designs for eating on the move). The Plakatraum (Poster Collection) across the road within Zurich's **Design School** (🅐 Limmatstr. 55) draws on an extensive archive of vintage posters for its temporary exhibitions.

🅐 Ausstellungsstr. 60 ☎ 043 446 67 67 🅦 www.museum-gestaltung.ch 🕐 Museum: 10.00–17.00 Tues–Sun (until 20.00 Wed), closed Mon. Plakatraum: 13.00–17.00 Tues–Fri & Sun, closed Sat & Mon 🚊 Tram: 4, 13 (Museum für Gestaltung) ℹ Admission charge

Schweizerisches Landesmuseum (Swiss National Museum)

One of Zurich's top museums, it contains the world's largest collection of Swiss historical and cultural artefacts. It documents Swiss civilisation from prehistory to the modern age in over 100 rooms, with special emphasis on prehistory and the Middle Ages. Highlights include children's toys, silverware, Renaissance globes, regional costumes and an impressive collection of artefacts from each of the country's cantons. 🅐 Museumsstr. 2

☎ 044 218 65 11 ⓦ www.musee-suisse.ch ⏰ 10.00–17.00 Tues–Sun
(till 19.00 Thur), closed Mon ⓝ Tram: 4, 11, 13, 14 (Bahnhofquai).
❶ Admission charge

RETAIL THERAPY

Einzigart Hidden in a small courtyard, 'Unique art' is an
entertaining design and furniture shop crammed with witty
gadgets and gizmos. It provides a showcase for designers to
present prototypes and individual pieces and is brilliant for
unusual gift ideas. ⓐ Josefstr. 36 ☎ 044 440 46 00
ⓦ www.einzigart.ch ⏰ 11.30–18.30 Tues–Fri, 10.00–17.00 Sat,
closed Sun & Mon ⓝ Tram: 4, 13 (Museum für Gestaltung)

Freitag Shop Zurich Surely the most unusual shop in town, the
Freitag tower is a veritable mini-skyscraper, built out of 17 freight
containers. It houses over 1,600 individually designed bags, wallets
and accessories in all colours, shapes and sizes. ⓐ Geroldstr. 17

🔺 Stylish bits and bobs at Einzigart

043 366 95 20 www.freitag.ch 11.00–19.30 Mon–Fri, 11.00–17.00 Sat, closed Sun S-Bahn: Hardbrücke; Bus: 72, 33 (Pfingstweidstrasse)

Transa Travel & Outdoor Zürich's best selection of good-value, outdoor clothing and quality travel equipment. Josefstr. 59 044 278 90 60 www.transa.ch 10.00–19.00 Mon–Fri, 09.00–17.00 Sat, closed Sun Tram: 4, 13 (Limmatplatz)

TAKING A BREAK

Lily's Stomach Supply £ ❶ A trendy noodle bar serving delicious pan-Asian cuisine at long, communal tables. Ideal for those on a budget. Try the Pakistani curry or the Japanese *yaki soba* noodles, washed down with beers from around the world. Langstr. 197 044 440 18 85 www.lilys.ch 11.00–24.00 Mon–Thur, 11.00–01.00 Fri & Sat, 15.00–24.00 Sun Tram: 4, 13 (Limmatplatz)

Steinfels Restaurant £ ❷ Young, trendy restaurant with delightful, 70s-feel interior design and international cuisine. Heinrichstr. 267 044 271 10 30 www.steinfels-zuerich.ch 11.00–00.30 Mon–Thur, 11.30–01.00 Fri, 14.00–01.00 Sat, 13.00–23.00 Sun Tram: 4, 13 (Escher-Wyss-Platz)

Swiss Museum Café £ ❸ Enjoy coffee and cake or a light lunch snack at this jazzy, minimalist café in the Landesmuseum. Museumsstr. 2 044 218 65 11 10.00–17.00 Tues–Sun, closed Mon Tram: 4, 11, 13, 14 (Bahnhofquai)

AFTER DARK

RESTAURANTS
Al Solito Posto £ ❹ This old-fashioned, family-run
Italian restaurant serves some of the best pizzas in town.
ⓐ Gasometerstr. 26 ❶ 044 272 62 92 ⏰ 11.30–14.00, 17.30–24.00
Mon–Fri, 18.00–24.00 Sat, closed Sun ⓝ Tram: 4, 13 (Limmatplatz)

Josef ££ ❺ Small, trendy restaurant, with stylish interior, superb
wine list and simple, Swiss-Italian menu. ⓐ Gasometerstr. 24
❶ 044 271 65 95 ⓦ www.josef.ch ⏰ 11.30–14.00, 18.30–23.00
Mon–Fri, 18.30–23.00 Sat, closed Sun ⓝ Tram: 4, 13 (Limmatplatz)

LaSalle £££ ❻ The unusual setting and artful modern European
cuisine draws Zurich's chic set here. ⓐ Schiffbaustr. 4 ❶ 044 258
70 71 ⓦ www.lasalle-restaurant.ch ⏰ 11.00–24.00 Mon & Tues,
11.00–01.00 Wed & Thur, 11.00–02.00 Fri, 17.00–02.00 Sat,
17.00–24.00 Sun ⓝ Tram: 4, 13 (Limmatplatz)

Sala of Tokyo £££ ❼ One of Switzerland's best Japanese
restaurants. Booking essential. ⓐ Limmatstr. 29 ❶ 044 271 52 90
ⓦ www.sala-of-tokyo.ch ⏰ 11.45–14.00, 18.00–22.45 Tues–Fri,
18.00–22.45 Sat, closed Sun & Mon ⓝ Tram: 4, 13 (Sihlquai)

BARS & CLUBS
Most of the district's nightlife is focused on trendy Limmatstrasse,
with a cluster of bars and clubs around Escher-Wyss Platz, too.

❶ *The Zürichsee with the Alps in the background*

OUT OF TOWN

trips

Lake Zurich (Zürichsee)

Lake Zurich offers an enormous choice of short excursions. Near the city, its shores are dominated by grassy parks, lakeside promenades and early 20th-century mansions. Further afield, picturesque villages such as Rapperswil and Küsnacht punctuate the shoreline, flanked by lush, green countryside and gentle hills – a veritable walker's paradise. Even the lake itself offers a wide variety of activities, including sailing, pleasure-boat cruising and swimming.

GETTING AROUND

The region is easy to explore by boat, on foot or on wheels.

By boat

The options are many: a day cruise to Rapperswil for lunch, museums and shopping; a morning cruise from Thalwil to Küsnacht for a lazy lakeside lunch; or escape the crowds and enjoy a relaxing stroll on the island of Ufenau. The **Zürichsee Schifffahrtsgesellschaft (ZSG)** (ⓐ Mythenquai 333 ⓘ 044 487 13 33 ⓦ www.zsg.ch) offers a variety of excursions from two-hour mini-cruises to full-day outings. During summer months, ZSG ferries stop at every lakeside town.

By bike

The lake region is also ideal for cyclists. You can either pedal around the lake (along the 'Seestrasse'), or ride a section of National Bike Route Number 9; called the 'Route des Lacs', this is

one of nine national bicycle touring routes, and it takes keen cyclists right across Switzerland from Lake Constance to Lake Geneva. Bikes are available for rental at train stations in Rapperswil, Ziegelbrücke and the Zurich Hauptbahnhof.
☎ 051 222 2904 🅦 www.rentabike.ch

By S-Bahn
The local train lines run the length of both shores, offering an easy, scenic journey to such destinations as Rapperswil and Küsnacht. Depending on the time you wish to travel, you may consider purchasing a 9-Uhr Tagespass (9 o'clock Daypass), valid after 09.00 Monday to Friday and all day Saturday and Sunday.

🔺 *Sailing on the Zürichsee*

OUT OF TOWN

SIGHTS & ATTRACTIONS

Alpamare

Europe's largest indoor water park, with ten thrilling water-slides, fun indoor and outdoor pools and wellness attractions too, including Switzerland's only iodine brine pool, thermal pools, whirlpools and saunas. ⓐ Gwattstr. 12, Pfäffikon ⓣ 055 415 15 15 ⓦ www.alpamare.ch ⓛ 10.00–22.00 Mon–Thur, 10.00–23.00 Fri & Sat, 10.00–22.00 Sun ⓝ S-Bahn: S2, S8 (Pfäffikon) ⓘ Admission charge

Knies Kinderzoo (Knies Children's Zoo)

Children adore this well-known children's zoo, where they can pet, stroke and feed many of the 300-plus animals here, marvel at the performing sea lions, and ride elephants, camels and ponies. ⓐ Oberseestr. 41, Rapperswil ⓣ 055 220 67 60 ⓦ www.knieskinderzoo.ch ⓛ 09.00–18.00 daily ⓝ S-Bahn: S5, S7, S15 (Rapperswil) ⓘ Admission charge

Küsnacht

The hamlet of Küsnacht basks on the Goldküste ('Gold Coast'), the fashionable eastern side of the lake, named after its golden afternoon sunshine and glorious sunsets. Since 1986, it has been home to American pop star Tina Turner. The main appeal of Küsnacht is its celebrated restaurant. It also marks the start of the Küsnachter Tobel, a beautiful 7-km (4½-mile) pathway through shady forest, with excellent lake vistas en route. The lido is popular during summer months.
ⓝ S-Bahn: S6, S16

Rapperswil

This atmospheric lakeside town is sometimes called the 'City of Roses', due to its numerous rose gardens. One of the most delightful gardens is designed for the blind, with highly fragranced specimens and information in Braille. Another lies within the 16th-century Capuchin monastery. Other highlights include the Knies Children's Zoo (see opposite), the Circus Museum and an impressive medieval castle that contains a small museum devoted to Switzerland's Polish community (ⓦ www.muzeum-polskie.org ◐ 13.00–17.00 daily Apr–Oct). Explore the narrow streets and alleys of the medieval old town and be sure to pause a while in Fischmarktplatz, the most picturesque square – open to the lake and fringed with café terraces and a small marina. ❸ Rapperswil Zürichsee Tourismus, Hintergasse 16 ❶ 0848 811 500 ◐ 08.30–12.00, 13.30–17.00 Mon–Fri, closed Sat & Sun ⓝ Hourly boat from Bürklipl. (duration two hours); S-Bahn: S5, S7 .S15 (Rapperswil)

Stäfa

The main attraction of this unremarkable town is that it is the lake's largest wine-producing community, located at the foot of the Pfannenstiel (pan handle) – the main vine-growing area of the canton – near the stunning 27.6-km (17-mile) **Pfannenstiel Panoramaweg** (Panoramic Footpath ⓦ www.zpp.ch). There are stunning views of the lake and the Alps along the path, protected wildlife and plants, and cosy restaurants to stop in for a break. Two wine paths also start in Stäfa, with information panels providing wine lovers with valuable facts and figures about the grapes and wine culture of the lake. ⓝ S-Bahn: S7

Ufenau

Escape the city hubbub and visit the tranquil island of Ufenau during your lake cruise. The largest of two islands in the lake and measuring just 750 m by 200 m (2,460 ft by 656 ft), it is a perfect place to relax and enjoy nature. Stroll round the perimeter, sunbathe, visit the St Peter and St Paul Church with

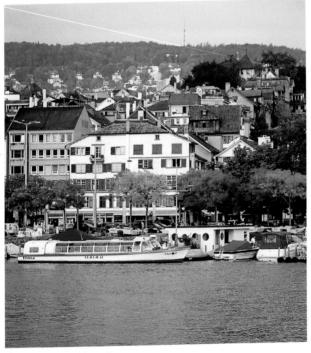

⬛ *Lake Zurich's 'Gold Coast'*

its 2nd-century Gallo-Romanic temple, or enjoy a meal at the self-service restaurant (🕐 Mar–Oct). Regrettably, swimming on the island is prohibited since it is a protected nature reserve. 🔘 www.ufenau.ch 🔘 Boat (see 🔘 www.zsg.ch)

Wädenswil

Winter is the best time to visit Wädenswil, when the natural outdoor ice-skating rink beside the lake is open. ❶ 043 477 91 51 🔘 www.eisbahnwaedi.ch 🕐 Check the website for rink's opening times 🔘 S-Bahn: S2, S8 (Wädenswil) ❶ Admission charge

CULTURE

Bergwerkmuseum Käpfnach (Coal Mining Museum)

Housed within an 18th-century coal storeroom, this unusual museum provides a rare glimpse into the history of coal mining and especially the miners' day-to-day life. 🔘 Bergwerkstr. 27, Horgen ❶ 044 725 39 35 🔘 www.bergwerk-kaepfnach.ch 🕐 13.00–16.30 Sat (Apr–Nov) 🔘 S-Bahn: S2, S8 ❶ Admission charge

Circus Museum Rapperswil

A fascinating insight into the history of Rapperswil's famous Knie family and its National Circus, its animal training and circus stunts, through colourful exhibits of original costumes, old posters, rare props and video films. Children especially enjoy trying on the old costumes in the 'kids' corner'. 🔘 Fischmarktpl. 1, Rapperswil ❶ 055 220 57 57 🕐 10.00–18.00 daily (Apr–June), 10.00–19.00 (July–Aug), 10.00–18.00 (Sept–Oct), 13.00–17.00 (Nov–Mar) 🔘 S-Bahn: S5, S7 (Rapperswil) ❶ Admission charge

FURTHER AFIELD

Atzmännig

Atzmännig is home to Switzerland's most exciting summer toboggan run. At 700 m (2,297 ft) long, its sharp bends, steep gradients and tunnels provide an adrenaline rush for all the family. In summer, there are wonderful country walks, while in winter, the snowy slopes are popular with skiers and snowboarders. ⓐ Sportbahnen Atzmännig, Goldingen ⓣ 055 284 64 34 ⓦ www.atzmaennig.ch ⓛ 10.00–11.45, 13.15–17.00 Mon–Fri, 08.30–17.15 Sat & Sun (Apr–May); 09.00–11.45, 13.15–17.15 Mon–Fri, 08.30–17.15 Sat & Sun (June–Sept); 09.00–11.45, 13.15–17.00 Mon–Fri; 09.00–17.00 Sat & Sun (Oct–Mar) ⓝ Train: Atzmännig

Einsiedeln

Less than an hour by train south of Lake Zurich, the town of Einsiedeln is the nation's most important pilgrimage site, drawing a quarter of a million devotees annually to its vast Kloster, the Baroque Benedictine Abbey. Its lavish interior contains a much-revered Black Madonna, and there are daily guided tours that provide a fascinating insight into the life of the monks and the history of the abbey.

Einsiedeln Tourismus ⓐ Hauptstr. 85, Einsiedeln ⓣ 055 418 44 88 ⓦ www.einsiedeln.ch ⓛ 09.00–12.00, 13.00–17.00 Mon–Fri, 09.00–12.00, 13.00–16.00 Sat, 10.00–13.00 Sun (Apr–Nov); 09.00–12.00 Sun (Dec–Mar)

Kloster Einsiedeln ⓐ Benzigerstr., Einsiedeln ⓣ 055 418 61 11 ⓦ www.kloster-einsiedeln.ch ⓛ Services 05.30–20.30 daily ⓝ Train: Einsiedeln (change at Wädenswil)

Hoch Ybrig

Zurich's nearest ski resort is easily accessible by train. In summer, hikers enjoy the idyllic landscape in the foothills of the Alps. In winter, it becomes a winter sports paradise, offering both downhill and cross-country skiing. The children's ski school is one of the best in Switzerland.

Ferien & Sportzentrum Hoch Ybrig ⓐ Waagtalstr. 127, Hoch Ybrig ⓣ 055 414 60 60 ⓦ www.hoch-ybrig.ch or www.ybrig.ch ⓝ Train: to Einsiedeln, then bus

TAKING A BREAK

Marsala ££ A smart, modern restaurant serving tasty Italian and Sicilian dishes near the harbour. ⓐ Seequai/Marktgasse 21, Rapperswil ⓣ 055 211 22 24 ⓦ www.marsala.ch ⓛ 11.00–14.30, 17.00–24.00 Mon–Fri, 11.00–24.00 Sat & Sun

Schützenhaus ££ A small, popular fish restaurant with beautiful views and alfresco dining, right on the lake. ⓐ Seestr. 48, Stäfa ⓣ 044 926 13 58 ⓦ www.schuetzenhaus-staefa.ch ⓛ 10.00–24.00 Thur–Mon, closed Tues & Wed

AFTER DARK

RESTAURANTS

Petermann's Kunststuben £££ Reputedly the best restaurant in Switzerland. Two-Michelin-starred Horst Petermann's inventive cuisine is served with elegance and artistic flair in an intimate dining room. ⓐ Seestr. 160, Küsnacht ⓣ 044 910 07 15

Ⓦ www.kunststuben.com Ⓒ 12.00–14.00, 19.00–21.00 Tues–Sat, closed Sun & Mon Ⓝ S-Bahn: S6, S16 (Küsnacht)

Schloss Rapperswil £££ Rapperswil's top restaurant, located within the castle, and best known for its sensational fish and seafood dishes. ☏ 055 210 18 28 Ⓦ www.schloss-restaurant.ch Ⓒ 11.30–23.30 Tues–Sat, 11.30–15.00 Sun, closed Mon

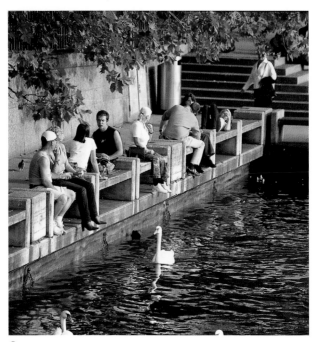

🔺 *Zürchers flock to the lake at weekends*

ACCOMMODATION

Camping Lützelau £ An idyllic campsite on the tiny island of Lützelau with barbecue and picnic areas, and a small restaurant. ⓐ Lützelau ⓣ 055 410 34 52 ⓦ www.luetzelau.ch ⓛ May–Sept ⓝ Island taxi boat (ⓣ 076 226 27 28): from Rapperswil

Jakob £ A popular choice at the heart of the old town, with 20 simple but stylish rooms, a classic bistro, trendy bar and beautiful vaulted wine cellar. ⓐ Hauptpl. 11, Rapperswil ⓣ 055 220 00 50 ⓦ www.jakob-hotel.ch

Hirschen-am-See ££ A friendly, country-style guesthouse on the lake, in the small village of Meilen, with two restaurants and panoramic views. ⓐ Seestr. 856, Obermeilen ⓣ 044 925 05 00 ⓦ www.hirschen-meilen.ch

Sonne ££ A romantic hotel in a beautiful location on the shore of the lake, with fine dining, fine art (paintings and sculptures by such artists as Tinguely and Warhol) and its very own beer garden and pier. ⓐ Seestr. 120, Küsnacht ⓣ 044 914 18 18 ⓦ www.sonne.ch

Lucerne (Luzern)

The city of Lucerne (Luzern in German) is every bit as picturesque as the postcards promise. With its remarkable blend of lakes, mountains, history, culture, folklore and architecture, this charming medieval town in central Switzerland has it all. Little wonder it is a tourist magnet.

Lucerne is located on the northern edge of Lake Lucerne (Vierwaldstättersee) at the foot of majestic Mount Pilatus, and is surrounded by spectacular alpine scenery steeped in

🔺 *The iconic Kapellbrücke*

the history of William Tell and the formation of the Swiss Confederation. The old quarter of town is located on the edge of the lake, and brims with charm and character. Its picturesque streets are dotted with historical monuments, fortifications and churches. The spacious riverbank promenades are ideal for strolling, and the breathtaking countryside is celebrated for its walks, panoramas, folklore and sports.

GETTING THERE

It takes just 50 minutes to reach Lucerne by train from the Zurich Hauptbahnhof (with departures every half hour). For further details of transport, sightseeing or accommodation, contact the Tourist Office:
Luzern Tourismus ⓐ Bahnhofstr. 3 ⓣ 041 227 17 17
ⓦ www.luzern.com

SIGHTS & ATTRACTIONS

Kapellbrücke (Chapel Bridge)
Europe's oldest covered wooden footbridge, spanning the Reuss River, is very much a symbol of Lucerne and the most photographed monument in Switzerland. Following a fire in 1993, it has undergone a major restoration project, including the reproduction of many of its remarkable Renaissance wall paintings.

Löwendenkmal (Lion Monument)
This world-famous monument – 'The Dying Lion of Lucerne' – was carved into the sandstone cliff above the town in 1821 to

commemorate the heroic deaths of Swiss mercenaries who died in Paris in 1792 trying to save the life of Marie Antoinette. Mark Twain described it as 'the saddest and most moving piece of rock in the world'. ⓐ Denkmalstr.

Mount Pilatus

The ascent of Mount Pilatus (2,132 m/6,993 ft), the giant, mystic mountain looming over Lucerne, is one of the most popular excursions in Switzerland. Until the 17th century, people were forbidden to climb it because locals feared that Pontius Pilate's ghost would bring about the downfall of Lucerne. According to legend, his body was brought here by the devil and his spirit haunts the summit.

Queen Victoria reached the top in 1868 on the back of a mule. Nowadays transportation is easier. Travel by nostalgic lake steamer from Lucerne to Alpnachstad and then with the world's steepest cogwheel railway, at a gradient of 48° (summer months only). Restaurants, a large sun terrace and dazzling 360° views over the Alps as far as Italy await you at the summit. Then travel via panoramic gondola and cable car (open all year) down to Kriens for the bus back to Lucerne. ⓐ Pilatus-Bahnen, Schlossweg 1, Kriens ⓣ 041 329 11 11 ⓦ www.pilatus.com

Mount Rigi

Lucerne's second major viewpoint (after Pilatus), and probably the most famous mountain view in Switzerland, Mount Rigi is called the 'island mountain' since it appears to be surrounded by the waters of lakes Lucerne, Zug and Lauerz. To reach the summit, take a boat from Lucerne to Vitznau, then a cogwheel train to

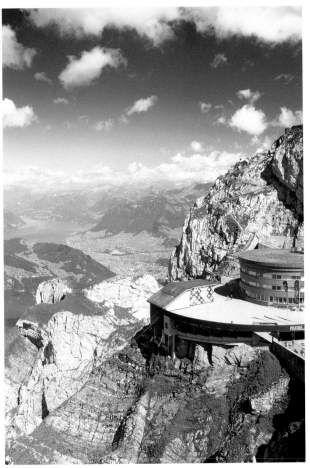

◯ *The summit of Mount Pilatus affords awesome views*

Rigi-Kulm, from where it is a 200-m (656-ft) walk to the summit. There are hiking trails all over the mountain, including several easy routes partway down to Rigi Kaltbad, where you can either pick up the cogwheel train or return by cable car to Weggis.

Museggmauer (Musegg Wall)
The ramparts of the medieval city wall yield magnificent views. The main section of the walk is from Wachtturm to the Zytturm, with the oldest clock in Lucerne, which bizarrely chimes one minute before all the others in town. ⓦ www.museggmauer.ch
🕐 08.00–19.00 daily (Easter–Oct) ❶ Admission charge

Vierwaldstättersee (Lake Lucerne, Lake of the Four Cantons)
The Vierwaldstättersee is one of the most beautiful lakes in Europe, situated at the meeting point of four cantons (Lucerne,

THE SWISS PATH
Der Weg der Schweiz ('The Swiss Path') is a special 37-km (23-mile) walkers' path around the southernmost part of Lake Lucerne (called Urnersee), designed in 1991 to celebrate 700 years of the Swiss Confederation. With sensational vistas, plenty of picnic areas and easy access by bus or boat from Lucerne, the walk can be done in various stages. Each section of the walk represents the individual cantons of Switzerland in the order that they joined the Confederation. The length of each canton's stretch represents the number of people living in that canton.

Uri, Unterwalden and Schwyz) with fjords that reach finger-like into the mountains. Its clear blue waters entice visitors for a swim or a trip on the nostalgic lake steamers to the various quaint villages dotted along its shores, including the idyllic villages of Gersau, Vitznau and Weggis, which form the 'Innerschweizer Riviera' on the sunny eastern shore of Lake Lucerne.

The surrounding chocolate-box scenery is Switzerland at its scenic best, with steep, tree-lined cliffs, lush alpine meadows, dense forests and snow-peaked mountains. Not only is this the heart of William Tell country, but it is also where the seeds of the Swiss Confederation were sown. It is a walkers' paradise, with numerous well-signposted trails, and cable cars and mountain railways for easy access to the upper slopes. There are also some excellent cycle trails. Ask at the tourist office for details: **Schifffahrtsgesellschaft des Vierwaldstättersees** ⓐ Werftestr. 5 ⓣ 041 367 67 67 ⓦ www.lakelucerne.ch

CULTURE

Kunstmuseum Luzern (Lucerne Art Museum)

Housed in the futuristic KKL Luzern building (see page 123), the Art Museum alternates selections from its permanent collection of Swiss 19th- and 20th-century art with temporary exhibitions of avant-garde contemporary art. Worth a visit for the building alone. ⓐ KKL, Europapl. 1 ⓣ 041 226 78 00 ⓦ www.kunstmuseumluzern.ch ⓛ 10.00–20.00 Tues & Wed, 10.00–18.00 Thur–Sun, closed Mon (Apr–late Nov); 10.00–20.00 Tues & Wed, 10.00–17.00 Thur–Sun, closed Mon (late Nov–Mar) ⓘ Admission charge

Sammlung Rosengart (Rosengart Collection)

An acclaimed art museum containing more than 200 works by
Cézanne, Chagall, Klee, Picasso, Matisse, Miró, Monet and others,
from the private collection of Lucerne art dealer Angela Rosengart.
ⓐ Pilatusstr. 10 ❶ 041 220 16 60 ⓦ www.rosengart.ch ⏰ 10.00–18.00
daily (Apr–Oct); 11.00–17.00 (Nov–Mar) ❶ Admission charge

Verkehrshaus der Schweiz (Swiss Transport Museum)

This impressive museum pays homage to Switzerland's
fascinating history of transport, telecommunications and tourism.
The exhibits include over 60 locomotives, 50 motorbikes and
every other type of transport imaginable. Space travel is
simulated in the Planetarium, and there's an IMAX cinema
showing documentary films. ⓐ Lidostr. 5 ❶ 041 370 44 44
ⓦ www.verkehrshaus.ch ⏰ 10.00–18.00 daily (Apr–Oct);
10.00–17.00 (Nov–Mar) ❶ Admission charge

RETAIL THERAPY

Bucherer The head office and largest branch of the leading
Swiss watch and jewellery retailer, with more than 4,000 items
for every taste and budget. ⓐ Schwanenpl. 5 ❶ 041 369 77 00
ⓦ www.bucherer.ch ⏰ 08.30–18.30 Mon, 09.00–18.30 Tues–Sat
(until 21.00 Thur); also 16.00–18.00 Sun (mid-Mar–Oct)

Carl Studer Vinothek Come here for expert advice and tastings
of fine Swiss wines. ⓐ Langensandstr. 7 ❶ 041 360 45 89
ⓦ www.studer-vinothek.ch ⏰ 10.00–12.00, 14.00–18.30 Tues–Fri,
10.00–16.00 Sat, closed Sun & Mon

Claudia Krebser Locally designed fashions for men and women in a stylish, old-town boutique. ⓐ Kauffmannweg 12 ⓣ 041 210 77 23 ⓦ www.claudiakrebser.com ⓛ 14.00–18.30 Mon, 09.00–12.30, 14.00–18.30 Tues–Fri, 10.00–16.00 Sat, closed Sun

Conditorei Heini Scrumptuous cakes and pâtisserie, including chocolate cows and 'Luzern Raindrops' (cherry-liqueur-filled chocolate drops). ⓐ Löwenpl. 9 ⓣ 041 412 20 20 ⓦ www.heini.ch ⓛ 06.00–18.30 Mon–Fri, 07.00–17.00 Sat, 09.00–17.00 Sun

Luzerner Wochenmarkt The sights, colours and fragrances of the market are a veritable feast for the senses. ⓐ River quays Bahnhofstr. & Jesuitenpl. ⓦ www.luzerner-wochenmarkt.ch ⓛ Tues & Sat 06.00–13.00

TAKING A BREAK

Kostgeberei £ Tasty organic cuisine in a simple yet stylish setting. Lunchtimes only. Excellent for vegetarians. ⓐ Ulmenstr. 14 ⓣ 041 360 34 13 ⓦ www.kostgeberei.ch ⓛ 11.30–14.00 Tues–Fri, closed Sat–Mon

AFTER DARK

RESTAURANTS

Taube £–££ Hearty home cooking in a rustic setting and the perfect place to sample local dishes. ⓐ Burgerstr. 3 ⓣ 041 210 07 47 ⓦ www.taube-luzern.ch ⓛ 11.00–00.30 Mon–Sat, closed Sun

⬤ *A twilight drink by the Reuss*

Bodu ££ Paris meets Lucerne at this classic brasserie, with excellent river views and regional French cuisine.
ⓐ Kornmarkt 5 ☎ 041 410 01 77 ⓦ www.brasseriebodu.ch
🕐 11.30–23.00 daily

Jasper £££ Inventive Michelin-starred Swiss cuisine accompanied by avant-garde décor and dazzling lake views.
ⓐ Haldenstr. 10 ☎ 041 416 16 16 ⓦ www.palace-luzern.com
🕐 12.00–14.00, 19.00–22.00 Wed–Mon, closed Tues

BARS & CLUBS
Pravda The hippest dance club in town, with excellent DJs.
ⓐ Pilatusstr. 29 ⓦ www.pravda.ch

Seeburg Lounge & Sunset City Beach A suave cocktail lounge for the beautiful people of Lucerne, with a midnight snack bar to keep you going into the early hours. The Sunset City Beach is the largest open-air bar in town, right on the lake.
ⓐ Seeburgstr. 53–61 ☎ 041 375 55 55 ⓦ www.hotelseeburg.ch

CONCERT VENUES
Kultur & Kongresszentrum Luzern (Lucerne Culture & Conference Centre) The stunning 'KKL' is an international masterpiece of modern architecture, created by French architect Jean Nouvel, with its roof jutting out far over its floor area and housing an art museum (see page 119) and concert hall with near-perfect acoustics. It is the venue of the celebrated Lucerne Festival – an international festival of music during summer.
ⓐ Europapl. 1 ☎ 041 226 70 70 ⓦ www.kkl-luzern.ch

ACCOMMODATION

Backpackers Lucerne £ A clean, cheap and friendly hostel by the lake, with family rooms, and also bikes and rollerblades for rent. ⓐ Alpenquai 42 ⓣ 041 360 04 20 ⓦ www.backpackerslucerne.ch

Magic £–££ Fun and quirky, each room here has a different theme, from Swiss chalet to Aladdin and even pirates. ⓐ Brandgässli 1 ⓣ 041 417 12 20 ⓦ www.magic-hotel.ch

Montana ££–£££ An opulent Art Deco hotel and day spa on a hill (reached by its own funicular), with breathtaking views across the lake and city to Mount Pilatus. ⓐ Adligenswilerstr. 22 ⓣ 041 419 00 00 ⓦ www.hotel-montana.ch

The Hotel £££ An ultra-modern boutique hotel in an old town house, designed by Jean Nouvel (of KKL fame, see pages 119 & 123). In each matt-black suite, a gigantic film scene adorns the ceiling. ⓐ Sempacherstr. 14 ⓣ 041 226 86 86 ⓦ www.the-hotel.ch

ⓞ *Greetings from sunny Zurich*

Zürich Schipfe

PRACTICAL
information

Directory

GETTING THERE

By air

Zurich's **Kloten Airport** (Ⓦ www.zurich-airport.com) is Switzerland's largest international airport and one of the busiest in Europe, serviced by over 100 different airlines, three-quarters of which offer scheduled services. Swiss International Air Lines, the national airline, is the main operator of scheduled flights to Switzerland from the UK and Europe, followed by British Airways, Lufthansa and Air France. Flights from the UK take less than hours to Zurich.

Information and online reservations can be made through the airlines' websites:

Air France Ⓦ www.airfrance.ch

American Airlines Ⓦ www.americanairlines.ch

British Airways Ⓦ www.britishairways.com

Delta Ⓦ www.delta.com

Lufthansa Ⓦ www.lufthansa.ch

Swiss Ⓦ www.swiss.com

Many people are aware that air travel emits CO_2, which contributes to climate change. You may be interested in the possibility of lessening the environmental impact of your flight through the charity **Climate Care** (Ⓦ www.jpmorganclimatecare.com), which offsets your CO_2 by funding environmental projects around the world.

By road

It is a long drive from the UK to Zurich, around 700 km (435 miles) from London. The usual route by car is through Belgium or the

Netherlands and then through Germany. An alternative route is through France, but tolls are payable on the French motorways. Before you enter Switzerland, you need to purchase a *vignette* (annual motorway tax, see page 56).

Coach travel is a reasonably priced option, with discounts for under 25s, senior citizens and those with disabilities. The journey from London Victoria takes around 18 hours. Contact **Eurolines** (ⓦ www.eurolines.com) for further information.

By rail
It's easy to travel from London to Zurich by train and it takes around 12 hours. Take the Eurostar to Paris via the Channel Tunnel, then a high-speed TGV train from Paris to Zurich. Contact Eurostar or Rail Europe for further information. For train times and fares within Switzerland, see the Swiss Federal Railways website.
Eurostar ⓦ www.eurostar.com
Rail Europe ⓦ www.raileurope.com
Swiss Federal Railways ⓦ www.sbb.ch

TRAVEL INSURANCE
It is important to take out adequate personal travel insurance for your city break, covering medical expenses, theft, loss, repatriation, personal liability and cancellation. If you are travelling in your own vehicle, you should also ensure that you have the appropriate insurance, and remember to pack the relevant insurance documents and your driving licence.

ENTRY FORMALITIES

Citizens of the UK, Republic of Ireland, other EU countries, the USA, Canada, Australia, New Zealand and South Africa are all permitted to enter Switzerland with a valid passport. A visa is required only if the duration of the stay is more than 90 days.

Visitors to Switzerland from Europe are entitled to bring 200 cigarettes, 50 cigars or 250 g of pipe tobacco. Visitors from non-European countries may import twice as much. The allowance for alcohol is the same for everyone: 1 litre of spirits and 2 litres of wine.

MONEY

Swiss currency is the Swiss franc (CHF), made up of 100 centimes (also called Rappen/centesimi in German/Italian-speaking regions). Notes are available in denominations of 10, 20, 50, 100, 500 and 1,000 francs, and coins are minted as 5, 10, 20 and 50 centimes, and also 1, 2 and 5 francs.

Fittingly, there are plenty of banks to choose from in Zurich. You can change money at banks, as well as at bureaux de change booths at the airport and the train station. ATMs are also common, accessible 24 hours a day, and have multilingual instructions. Most international bank or credit cards are accepted if you wish to withdraw Swiss francs, provided you know your PIN. Credit cards are widely accepted throughout the city, especially EuroCard and MasterCard.

HEALTH, SAFETY & CRIME

Zurich's water is safe to drink, as is the water from most of the city's fountains. The city's food presents no health risks.

The quality of healthcare in Zurich is generally very high. There is no free state health service in Switzerland, but thanks to a reciprocal agreement, citizens of the UK and other EU countries are entitled to reduced-cost, sometimes free, medical treatment on presentation of a valid European Health Insurance Card (EHIC – apply online at ⓦ www.dh.gov.uk/travellers). On top of this, private medical insurance is still advised and is essential for all non-EU visitors.

Zurich is essentially a safe city but, although crime rates are relatively low, it is advisable to take the same common-sense precautions against petty crime as you would in any major city: don't carry excess cash; use the hotel safe for valuable goods; beware of pickpockets in crowded places; and stick to well-lit, populated areas by night. See Emergencies section for police details (page 136).

OPENING HOURS

Museum and gallery opening times vary. Many open on Sunday and close for at least one day a week, often on Monday. Most shops open at least 09.30–18.30 Monday to Friday, and 08.30–16.00 or 17.00 on Saturday. Many stay open for late-night shopping until 20.00 on Thursday. Restaurants usually open 12.00–14.00 and 18.00–22.00, and are at their busiest around 20.30. Bank hours vary, but are generally 08.30–16.30 Monday to Friday (until 18.00 Thursday).

TOILETS

Public toilets charging CHF 1 or CHF 2 are generally pretty clean and can be found at all central points, including the

Hauptbahnhof (also with showering facilities), Bellevueplatz and Paradeplatz. They are open daily, usually 05.00–24.00.

CHILDREN

Zurich is a great place to bring kids. There are plenty of attractions to keep them amused, including – be warned – some wonderful toy shops. Restaurants and cafés will generally be happy to cater for children and some offer special menus or portions. When it comes to day-to-day maintenance, nappies, baby food and formula milk can all readily be bought in supermarkets.

One place that's bound to transport your progeny into a state of fluffy tranquility is Zoo Zurich (see page 81). Indeed, there's fun for all the family at this world-class – and ethically focused – zoo. Older children will adore the learning experience of the Masoala rainforest, while the Zoolino petting area is especially popular with toddlers. Zurich is circus-crazy, with various big-top bonanzas throughout the year. The best is undoubtedly the world-renowned Swiss National Circus **Knie** (ⓦ www.knie.ch), with its famous elephant, horse and seal acts – not to mention the clowns.

Childen aged 6 and upwards may enjoy the kids' tours at the Observatory on the first Saturday of each month at 15.00, 16.00 and 17.00 (ⓐ Uraniastr. 9 ⓣ 043 317 16 40 ⓦ www.urania-sternwarte.ch). Take the young ones for an eye-opening mooch around the free **Spielzeugmuseum** (Zurich Toy Museum, ⓐ Fortunagasse 15 ⓣ 044 211 93 05), which has a fascinating collection of antique toys from all over Europe. There are plenty of great places in and around Zurich for children to grab a slice

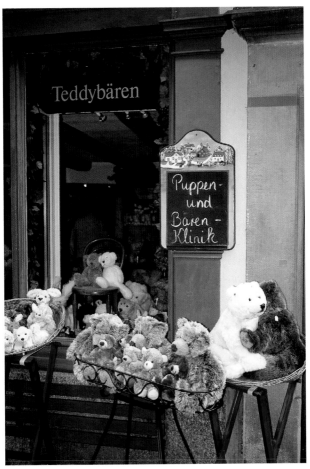

Children will find it hard to resist the charms of a furry friend of healthy exercise. Alpamare (see page 106) is a fantastic water park where the whole family will have a splashing time, with indoor and outdoor pools and crazy slides. The **Dolder Ice Skating Rink** (ⓐ Adlisbergstr. 36 ⓦ www.doldersports.com) is another great place for a family outing. There are even mini 'push-penguins' to help the little ones along and have fun while they gain confidence.

This generally child-friendly city has wonderful playgrounds, some of the best of which can be found in Fortunagasse (just beneath Lindenhof), beside the China Garden at Zürichhorn, and on the corner of Spiegelgasse and Untere Zäune in Niederdorf. Older children will enjoy cycling around the city, and you can hire a bike for free from Zürirollt (see page 53). Of course, nature has provided an incomparably family-friendly attraction in the shape of Lake Zurich (see page 65). Whether you take a traditional steamboat excursion, hire a bicycle or a pedalo, picnic on the shore, go for a bit of a trek or simply swim at one of the lidos, there's plenty to keep all the family amused here – and what an ideal location for snapping some ace holiday photos. If you love to go a-wandering along the mountain track, take the kids up Uetliberg (see page 65) for some fresh mountain air and exercise. Older children in particular will enjoy the 'Planets Trail', a two-hour hike from Uetliberg to Felsenegg, with its truly impressive models of the planets, made on a scale of 1:1 billion.

COMMUNICATIONS

Internet

For those who can't live without email, many hotels offer Internet and WLAN access, and there are Internet cafés around the city, too, although these tend to be quite expensive. Most public phone boxes have an electronic phonebook, which enables you to send short emails worldwide.

Internet Café Urania ⓐ Uraniastr. 3 ❶ 044 210 33 11 Ⓦ www.cafe.ch
🕐 07.00–23.00 Mon–Fri, 08.00–23.00 Sat, 10.00–22.00 Sun

Phone

The city's trendy new public phones (Ⓦ www.swisscom.com) are easy to spot – stylish glass-and-granite cylinders that glow pink at night. They are also straightforward to use, with instructions in English. Basically, lift the handset, insert payment then dial the number. They take major credit cards (VISA, MasterCard, Amex, Diners Club and JCB) and the following coins: CHF 1, CHF 2 and CHF 5, plus 10, 20 and 50 centimes.

For reverse charge/collect calls to the USA, Canada, Japan, UK and Australia and worldwide calls with a credit card, dial ❶ 0800 265 532, wait for the prompt and dial 1 for English or 0 for the operator.

TELEPHONING SWITZERLAND
The city area code for Zurich is 044. If calling Zurich from abroad, dial the country code 41 for Switzerland, drop the first zero, press 4-4 and then the rest of the number.

TELEPHONING ABROAD
Dial 00, the country code, the area code and the local number. Dialling codes: Australia 61; Canada 1; Ireland 353; New Zealand 64; South Africa 27; UK 44; USA 1.

Post

There are three ways to send your mail from Switzerland:
Urgent (for same-day or next-day international deliveries),
Airmail (Europe) and Airmail (rest of world).
Sihlpost (Main Post Office) ⓐ Kasernenstr. 95–97
🕐 06.30–22.30 Mon–Fri, 06.30–20.00 Sat, 10.00–22.30 Sun
Swiss Post ⓦ www.swisspost.ch

ELECTRICITY

The electricity supply in Zurich is 220 V, 50 Hz. Swiss sockets
are generally recessed, and plugs are round, flat or hexagonally
shaped with two pins. British and US appliances need a plug
adaptor, and North American appliances also need a
transformer.

TRAVELLERS WITH DISABILITIES

Switzerland is well prepared to receive travellers with disabilities
and the facilities are generally of a high standard. The following
are useful resources:
**Behinderten Transport Zurich (Zurich Transport for the
Physically Disabled)** provides a 24-hour bus service for
passengers in wheelchairs. ☏ 044 444 22 11 ⓦ www.btz.ch
Disabled Persons Transport Advisory Committee (UK)
ⓦ www.dptac.gov.uk/door-to-door
Mobility International Switzerland (MIS) ☏ 062 206 88 35
ⓦ www.mis-ch.ch
Switzerland Tourism publishes a useful hotel guide specifically
for visitors with disabilities. ⓦ www.myswitzerland.com

TOURIST INFORMATION

Zurich's Tourist Information Office is located at the **Hauptbahnhof** (main train station) and is a useful source for maps, attractions and event information and any other queries you have about the city and the rest of Switzerland. It also offers a hotel reservation service. ⓐ Hauptbahnhof ⓣ 044 215 40 00 ⓕ 044 215 40 44 ⓦ www.zuerich.com ⓛ 08.00–19.00 Mon–Sat, 08.00–12.00, 13.00–17.00 Sun

BACKGROUND READING

There are surprisingly few books solely about Zurich, and very few Swiss authors have been translated into English. Novels featuring the city include:

Small g: A Summer Idyll by Patricia Highsmith. Lives and loves in a gay bar in Zurich.

The Bourne Identity by Robert Ludlum. A thriller set in Marseille, Zurich and Paris of the 1970s.

The Pieces from Berlin by Michael Pye. Wartime reflections, set in Zurich.

Emergencies

EMERGENCY NUMBERS
Police ❶ 117
Fire ❶ 118
Ambulance ❶ 144
Crisis line ❶ 143
24-hour doctor (Ärtzefon) ❶ 044 421 21 21

MEDICAL SERVICES
Should you become seriously ill, lists of local doctors, dentists and hospitals can be found in telephone directories or by contacting your consulate, which has lists of English-speaking practitioners. Alternatively, ask your hotel reception to help or, in a real emergency, dial ❶ 144.

Zurich has one of the best healthcare systems in the world with modern, well-equipped hospitals and superb nursing care. If you have a valid European Health Insurance Card (EHIC, see page 129) you will be entitled to cheaper, sometimes free, medical treatment. However, dental care, except emergency accident treatment, is not available free of charge.

24-hour pharmacy, Bellevue Apotheke ❸ Theaterstr. 14
❶ 044 266 62 22 🅦 www.bazh.com Ⓝ Tram: 2, 4, 5, 8, 9, 11, 15 (Bellevue)

Universitätspital (University Hospital) The main city hospital with over 1,000 beds and an accident centre. ❸ Rämistr. 100
❶ 044 255 11 11 Ⓝ Tram: 6, 9, 10 (ETH/Universitätsspital)

University of Zurich Dental Clinic ❸ Plattenstr. 11 ❶ 044 634 33 11
Ⓝ Tram: 5, 6 (Platte)

EMERGENCY PHRASES

Help!	**Fire!**	**Stop!**
Hilfe!	Feuer!	Halt!
Hilfer!	*Foyer!*	*Halt!*

Please call an ambulance/a doctor/the police/the fire service!
Rufen Sie bitte einen Krankenwagen/einen Arzt/
die Polizei/die Feuerwehr!
Roofen zee bitter inen krankenvaagen/inen artst/
dee politsye/dee foyervair!

POLICE

Kantonspolizei Zurich (Cantonal Police Station)
ⓐ Hauptbahnhof ☎ 044 247 22 11
Stadtpolizei Zurich (City Police Station) ⓐ Bahnhofquai 3
☎ 044 411 71 17 (24-hour service)

EMBASSIES & CONSULATES

Australia ⓐ Chemins des Fins 2, Geneva ☎ 022 799 91 00
Canada ⓐ Kirchenfeldstr. 88, Bern ☎ 031 357 32 00
New Zealand ⓐ Chemins des Fins 2, Geneva ☎ 022 929 03 50
Republic of Ireland ⓐ Claridenstr. 25, Zurich ☎ 044 289 25 15
South Africa ⓐ Alpenstr. 29, Bern ☎ 031 350 13 13
UK ⓐ Gämsenstr. 3, Zurich ☎ 044 383 65 60
USA ⓐ Dufourstr. 101, Zurich ☎ 043 499 29 60

ACKNOWLEDGEMENTS

The publishers would like to thank the following individuals and organisations for supplying their copyright photographs for this book: Jari Aherma/Fotolia, page 114; Chris Brown, page 34; Chris Devers, page 13; World Pictures/Photoshot, pages 117, 122; Teresa Fisher, all others.

Project editor: Jennifer Jahn
Layout: Trevor Double
Copy editor: Paul Hines
Proofreaders: Cath Senker & Caroline Hunt

Teresa Fisher would like to thank Switzerland Tourism (ⓦ www.myswitzerland.com), Zurich Tourism (ⓦ www.zuerich.com), George Downing and Emmanuel Vermot for their help in the preparation of this book.

Send your thoughts to
books@thomascook.com

* **Found a great bar, club, shop or must-see sight that we don't feature?**

* **Like to tip us off about any information that needs a little updating?**

* **Want to tell us what you love about this handy little guidebook and more importantly how we can make it even handier?**

Then here's your chance to tell all! Send us ideas, discoveries and recommendations today and then look out for your valuable input in the next edition of this title.

Email the above address (stating the title) or write to:
pocket guides Series Editor, Thomas Cook Publishing, PO Box 227, Coningsby Road, Peterborough PE3 8SB, UK.

WHAT'S IN YOUR GUIDEBOOK?

Independent authors Impartial up-to-date information from our travel experts who meticulously source local knowledge.

Experience Thomas Cook's 165 years in the travel industry and guidebook publishing enriches every word with expertise you can trust.

Travel know-how Thomas Cook has thousands of staff working around the globe, all living and breathing travel.

Editors Travel-publishing professionals, pulling everything together to craft a perfect blend of words, pictures, maps and design.

You, the traveller We deliver a practical, no-nonsense approach to information, geared to how you really use it.

Useful phrases

English	German	Approx pronunciation
BASICS		
Yes	Ja	*Yah*
No	Nein	*Nine*
Please	Bitte	*Bitter*
Thank you	Danke schön	*Danker shern*
Hello	Hallo	*Hallo*
Goodbye	Auf Wiedersehen	*Owf veederzeyhen*
Excuse me	Entschuldigen Sie	*Entshuldigen zee*
Sorry	Entschuldigung	*Entshuldigoong*
That's okay	Das stimmt	*Das shtimt*
I don't speak German	Ich spreche kein Deutsch	*Ikh shprekher kine doitsh*
Do you speak English?	Sprechen Sie Englisch?	*Shprekhen zee eng-lish?*
Good morning	Guten Morgen	*Gooten morgen*
Good afternoon	Guten Tag	*Gooten tagh*
Good evening	Guten Abend	*Gooten aabent*
Goodnight	Gute Nacht	*Goote naakht*
My name is ...	Mein Name ist ...	*Mine naamer ist ...*
NUMBERS		
One	Eins	*Ines*
Two	Zwei	*Tsvy*
Three	Drei	*Dry*
Four	Vier	*Feer*
Five	Fünf	*Foonf*
Six	Sechs	*Zex*
Seven	Sieben	*Zeeben*
Eight	Acht	*Akht*
Nine	Neun	*Noyn*
Ten	Zehn	*Tseyn*
Twenty	Zwanzig	*Tvantsikh*
Fifty	Fünfzig	*Foonftsikh*
One hundred	Hundert	*Hoondert*
SIGNS & NOTICES		
Airport	Flughafen	*Floogharfen*
Train station	Bahnhof	*Baanhof*
Platform	Bahnsteig	*Baanshtykh*
Smoking/non-smoking	Rauchen/	*Raukhen/*
	rauchen verboten	*Raukhen ferboten*
Toilets	Toiletten	*Toletten*
Ladies/Gentlemen	Damen/Herren	*Daamen/Herren*
Bus	Bus	*Booss*